EVEN NOW ...

THE RESURRECTION OF YOUR HOPES AND DREAMS

LEE SHIPP

Copyright © 2009 by Lee Shipp

Even Now …
The Resurrection of Your Hopes and Dreams
by Lee Shipp

Printed in the United States of America

ISBN 9781615793082

All rights reserved solely by the author. The author guarantees all contents are original and do not infringe upon the legal rights of any other person or work. No part of this book may be reproduced in any form without the permission of the author. The views expressed in this book are not necessarily those of the publisher.

Unless otherwise indicated, Bible quotations are taken from The Holy Bible: King James Version.

www.xulonpress.com

OTHER BOOKS
BY PASTOR LEE SHIPP

God is Not Dead and Neither Am I
(Available through First New Testament Church).

Why Live This Way ... When You Don't Have To?
(Available through Xulon Press, Barnes and Noble, Amazon.com, and First New Testament Church).

DEDICATION

To Mary and Martha ... They rolled the stone away and gave all of us hope!

ACKNOWLEDGEMENTS

I am very blessed to have such willing and capable people who have taken on this project and carried it through to its finished form. First of all, to my wife, Carla, who has read and re-read the manuscripts, encouraging me on the content and the power of the message. To Mary Currier, who proofed the work and helped with much needed corrections. And lastly to Janice McCoy, who painstakingly examined every word in order that the book might flow smoothly from the pages into your heart. You all are a God-send to me. Your help is so valuable and I am convinced this book would not be worthy of publishing if it were not for your help!

TABLE OF CONTENTS

INTRODUCTION	The Goodness of God	xvii
CHAPTER ONE	Even Now … I Need A Savior	27
CHAPTER TWO	Even Now … In The Name of God	33
CHAPTER THREE	Even Now … When I Need A Miracle	45
CHAPTER FOUR	Even Now … What Defines You	57
CHAPTER FIVE	Even Now … When I Don't Feel Like It	73
CHAPTER SIX	Even Now … When I Have Lost All Hope	85
CHAPTER SEVEN	Even Now … Has Sin Destroyed My Future	99
CHAPTER EIGHT	Even Now … When Living Seems Impossible	113
CHAPTER NINE	Even Now … When I Want To Quit	129
CHAPTER TEN	Even Now … When I Need a Breakthrough	141
CHAPTER ELEVEN	Even Now … In A Valley	155
CHAPTER TWELVE	Even Now … God Does Love Me	171
About The Author		187

John 11:1 - 44

¹Now a certain *man* was sick, *named* Lazarus, of Bethany, the town of Mary and her sister Martha. ²(It was *that* Mary which anointed the Lord with ointment, and wiped his feet with her hair, whose brother Lazarus was sick.) ³Therefore his sisters sent unto him, saying, Lord, behold, he whom thou lovest is sick. ⁴When Jesus heard *that*, he said, This sickness is not unto death, but for the glory of God, that the Son of God might be glorified thereby. ⁵Now Jesus loved Martha, and her sister, and Lazarus. ⁶When he had heard therefore that he was sick, he abode two days still in the same place where he was. ⁷Then after that saith he to *his* disciples, Let us go into Judaea again. ⁸*His* disciples say unto him, Master, the Jews of late sought to stone thee; and goest thou thither again? ⁹Jesus answered, Are there not twelve hours in the day? If any man walk in the day, he stumbleth not, because he seeth the light of this world. ¹⁰But if a man walk in the night, he stumbleth, because there is no light in him. ¹¹These things said he: and after that he saith unto them, Our friend Lazarus sleepeth; but I go, that I may awake him out of sleep. ¹²Then said his disciples, Lord, if he sleep, he shall do well. ¹³Howbeit Jesus spake of his death: but they thought that he had spoken of taking of rest in sleep. ¹⁴Then said Jesus unto them plainly, Lazarus is dead. ¹⁵And I am glad for your sakes that I was not there, to the intent ye may believe; nevertheless let us go unto him. ¹⁶Then said Thomas, which is called Didymus, unto his fellowdisciples, Let us also go, that we may die with him. ¹⁷Then when Jesus came, he found that he had *lain* in the grave four days already. ¹⁸Now Bethany was nigh unto Jerusalem, about fifteen furlongs off: ¹⁹And

Even Now ...

many of the Jews came to Martha and Mary, to comfort them concerning their brother. [20]Then Martha, as soon as she heard that Jesus was coming, went and met him: but Mary sat *still* in the house. [21]Then said Martha unto Jesus, Lord, if thou hadst been here, my brother had not died. [22]But I know, that even now, whatsoever thou wilt ask of God, God will give *it* thee. [23]Jesus saith unto her, Thy brother shall rise again. [24]Martha saith unto him, I know that he shall rise again in the resurrection at the last day. [25]Jesus said unto her, I am the resurrection, and the life: he that believeth in me, though he were dead, yet shall he live: [26]And whosoever liveth and believeth in me shall never die. Believest thou this? [27]She saith unto him, Yea, Lord: I believe that thou art the Christ, the Son of God, which should come into the world. [28]And when she had so said, she went her way, and called Mary her sister secretly, saying, The Master is come, and calleth for thee. [29]As soon as she heard *that*, she arose quickly, and came unto him. [30]Now Jesus was not yet come into the town, but was in that place where Martha met him. [31]The Jews then which were with her in the house, and comforted her, when they saw Mary, that she rose up hastily and went out, followed her, saying, She goeth unto the grave to weep there. [32]Then when Mary was come where Jesus was, and saw him, she fell down at his feet, saying unto him, Lord, if thou hadst been here, my brother had not died. [33]When Jesus therefore saw her weeping, and the Jews also weeping which came with her, he groaned in the spirit, and was troubled, [34]And said, Where have ye laid him? They said unto him, Lord, come and see. [35]Jesus wept. [36]Then said the Jews, Behold how he loved him! [37]And some of them said, Could not this man, which opened the eyes of the blind, have caused that even this man should not have died? [38]Jesus therefore again groaning in himself cometh to the grave. It was a cave, and a stone lay upon it. [39]Jesus said, Take ye away the stone. Martha, the sister of him that was dead, saith unto him, Lord, by this time he stinketh: for he hath been *dead* four days. [40]Jesus saith unto her, Said I not unto thee, that, if thou wouldest believe, thou shouldest see the glory of God? ⁴¹Then they took away the stone *from the place* where the dead was laid. And Jesus lifted up *his* eyes, and said, Father, I thank thee that thou hast heard me. ⁴²And I knew that thou hearest me always: but because of the people which stand by I said *it*, that they may believe that thou hast sent me. ⁴³And when he thus had spoken, he cried with a loud voice, Lazarus, come forth. ⁴⁴And he that was dead came forth, bound hand and foot with graveclothes: and his face was bound about with a napkin. Jesus saith unto them, Loose him, and let him go.

INTRODUCTION

EVEN NOW ... THE GOODNESS OF GOD

"Oh, taste and see that the Lord is good; Blessed is the man who trusts in Him!" (Psalm 34:8). Be honest; now what do you actually live about God? No, you did not read that question wrong; what do you "live" about God? Though theologically we cringe at the suggestion "God is bad," sometimes the way we live gives the impression that God cannot be trusted or His goodness counted on.

Though we may believe correctly in our minds, we may not allow that belief to influence the way we live. An honest answer would cause all of us to admit that we have voiced complaints to God for things He has allowed into our lives. We have accused him, by our actions, not by our theology, of being unkind. We have questioned his faithfulness and we have even questioned whether the Heavenly **FATHER** even cares for us. Surely Mary and Martha must had wondered about God's faithfulness when their brother Lazarus died.

I was arrested by Martha's faith. The drama of Lazarus' illness had concluded, the curtain was drawn ... Lazarus was in the grave ... Mary and Martha were devastated ... and it appeared Jesus failed! How does a woman approach God when her brother has been in the grave for four days? That was the question I had to ask. At first she approached Him as I probably would, somewhat upset, "Lord if you had been here ..." I can hear the disappointment in her voice. I read it in her words. At that moment I wondered how many times I have approached God like that. I just suspected that He had failed me. I thought my dreams were over. How many times have you approached God that way? How many dreams have you buried?

But Martha went on to say something that echoed in my being, something that many believers do not do today. With the gloom of death prevailing over the gathering, the sounds of mourners weeping, and the grave of her beloved brother in sight she said something remarkable, "But I know, that even now, whatsoever thou wilt ask of God, God will give *it* thee" (John 11:21 – 22).

GOD'S LOVE NEVER FAILS

Wow! Is it possible that we have kept our dreams and hopes shut up in the grave because we could not get passed the feelings of disappointment to say to God, "But Even Now …?"

Our world is filled with the cries of suffering people. The night rings with the groaning of a wife who lies beside a husband she fears no longer loves her. A father is restless as he waits for his wayward son to come home safe.

Satan has zapped our hope! He has launched a massive attack on our joy, but Jesus is coming to the rescue. That's right! Please quit thinking it's over. Jesus is coming! He will not be too late (even if your dreams are buried); He is coming to help you!

In this book I have taken the episodes that Satan uses the most to show you that it is never over! Not even personal sin and shame can prevent the Redeeming God from opening up your tombs and bringing fresh hope to your failing heart!

Satan has tried to imprison us into believing that God has failed us. But He has not. That is what I want you to know. God has not failed you. Maybe He did not come when you wanted, but He has come – He has come to help you. Please do not say it is too late. What would have happened if Martha had said that? It does not matter how long it has been; the fact that you hold this book in your hands is the evidence that God has come. He will speak to you here. He will encourage you to believe. He will assure you that if you will believe you will see the Glory of God.

LIVING BY FAITH IS NOT EASY BUT IT IS NECESSARY

It was not easy for Martha. She would have to interrupt the funeral. And she would do this based upon the instructions of a man who not only failed to heal her brother, but also failed to come to the funeral! Martha's faith that day was crucial for the miracle to occur. Martha, why are you going to listen to Jesus? Are you really going to roll the stone away? Come on Martha, you gave Jesus a chance and He failed. No one would blame you if you told Jesus, "No." Thank God, Martha had faith in Jesus – faith in His love and faith in His ability! She did not throw her confidence away. She did not turn back. With every emotional pain and confusion stretched to its limit, with every reason not to have faith, with Lazarus' corpse decaying in the tomb, she said to Jesus, "Even Now, whatever you ask the Father He will give that to you." How could she do that? Because she believed in Him! And as soon as Martha told the men, "Remove the stone," Lazarus came out.

Do you believe that God is good only as long as He is doing what you want Him to do; or do you believe God is good even when you are faced with circumstances that throw you into confusion, and it seems to you that God is so far away?

How many times have people considered God's "absence" as God's failure to care about them? How many have mistaken the fact that when God did not do what they wanted, when they wanted, then God failed and let them down; and unlike Martha and Mary, their disappointment caused them to miss the miracle God intended to bring all along?

As Martha, can you remove the self imposed barriers barring you from God's ordained destiny? What is it that has sealed your fate or robbed you of your dreams? Can you roll it away?

However, I know what some are thinking. We have all thought it. We have thought it because we all had to deal with it. You know what I am referring to! Those times in our life when we really trusted God, but He didn't answer. The help did not come! So some of you are reading this saying, "I want to trust God but it is hard. I have trusted before and it did not appear that God was faithful to me."

WHY YOU SHOULD READ THIS BOOK

This book will answer that question! This book reveals the power and faithfulness of God to take us past the most impossible circumstances of life. Rooted firmly in the Bible, this book will show you how God can take you past the most heinous issues of your life:

... The loss of hope,

... The devastation of sin,

... The paralysis of raw emotions,

... The aching suspicions of God's faithfulness and love,

... And so much more.

This Book will encourage you to roll your stones away, so God may resurrect your buried dreams and hopes! An "Even Now" situation is not limited to the passing of a loved one or a feeling of abandonment by God. An "Even Now" moment is any tragedy or circumstance that makes you feel hopeless. It is those times when your dreams become nightmares and visions have slipped away.

If you are walking in God's will and trusting in God, He will never allow anything to destroy you. You may think something is going to kill you. You may even want to die, but you will not! God wants your faith to grow! And how does your faith grow? By God delivering you! Why do you trust God? Because He proves trustworthy! He is not going to let you be ashamed! He is showing you to trust Him. He is showing you His way.

Regardless of our actions, the Bible clearly declares the goodness of God. The testimony of tried saints is that God is good! When the Bible states that God is good it is saying that He is favorable, pleasing, and festive! The goodness of God is that which disposes Him to be kind, cordial, benevolent, and full of good will toward men. He is tenderhearted and of quick sympathy; and His unfailing attitude toward all moral beings is open, frank, and friendly. By His nature He is inclined to bestow blessedness, and He takes holy pleasure in the happiness of His people.

WE WILL TASTE THE GOODNESS OF GOD

God's goodness is practical. Just as God intends for us to do good to all men and to treat others as we would want to be treated, even so are the acts of God's goodness to man. David said to "taste." Don't merely consider it as a theological concept. The invitation is not to a mystical application but a practical display. Moses tells us that the display of God's goodness is not rare but a lavish pouring out to all men continually, "The Lord, the Lord God, merciful and gracious, longsuffering and *abounding in goodness* and truth..."

To better grasp the goodness of God it would be helpful to understand what the opposite of good is. If someone were bad, this would mean they would know what is right, had the power to perform the right, yet neglected to do it. If God is good, then He acts in our behalf to do what He knows is best. Because God is all-knowing, He knows what is best. This means everything! This view of God brings peace for the one who believes it; the one who knows that nothing can go wrong under His care. If the Lord is good, He will not neglect His duties to us; and if we believe in His goodness, we would never accuse Him of evil the next time we are in trouble!

So how do we reconcile the fact that a good God would allow His people to suffer? We are not the only ones to battle this question; the great prophet Jeremiah did as well. In chapter twenty, verses seven through eight he says, "O Lord, You induced me, and I was persuaded; You are stronger than I, and have prevailed. I am in derision daily; Everyone mocks me. For when I spoke, I cried out; I shouted, 'Violence and plunder!' Because the word of the Lord was made to me a reproach and a derision daily." Prophet or not he's in a struggle. But you don't have to be a prophet with the whole nation hating you to have these thoughts.

Many have battled with these same thoughts. How could the Lord allow this in my life? Why would He allow my marriage to fall apart? He is mighty to save, so why doesn't He save my children?

I am trying so hard to please Him and live for Him, but right now I can not bring myself to pray, "Thy will be done." In Jeremiah 20:9-11, God's goodness comes through:

> Then I said, 'I will not make mention of Him, Nor speak anymore in His name.' But His word was in my heart like a burning fire shut up in my bones; I was weary of holding it back, and I could not. For I heard many mocking: 'Fear on every side!' 'Report,' they say, 'and we will report it!' All my acquaintances watched for my stumbling, saying, 'Perhaps he can be induced; Then we will prevail against him, And we will take our revenge on him.' But the Lord is with me as a mighty, awesome One. Therefore my persecutors will stumble, and will not prevail. They will be greatly ashamed, for they will not prosper. Their everlasting confusion will never be forgotten.

Directly from God came this strong surge of hope and confidence.

God would not let him go. Even when Jeremiah was weak and scared and confused as to what God was doing, God held him and would not let him go. Oh, Hallelujah! What a good God! There were times our feet had almost slipped, but He kept us from falling!

I learn from Jeremiah that it is important to be open with God about my thoughts and feelings. It is in the midst of great turmoil that the revelation of what I believe about God really comes forth. Many are the times my weaknesses are evident. Just when I think I trust Him He let's me see how little I rest in Him. If it were not for the trials which revealed my little faith and lack of trust in God then I would have never moved on to greater faith; even this is the goodness of God!

These thoughts that go unconfessed will create great damage in our relationship with God. We may try to deny bad thoughts and feelings about God, but try as we may to ignore them they will create a gulf of doubt and unbelief in our hearts. Such unconfessed thoughts will eventually leave us bitter and hardened to the awesome life God had in store for us.

Even Now ...

Let your faith rest in God. Though you may be in the midst of confusion and turmoil believe that God is good, and no matter how it looks He will do what is right in your life. It is foolish to be troubled when you know God is good, and His ways are right!

"My God, I have never thanked Thee for my thorns.

I have thanked Thee a thousand times for my roses,

But not once for my thorns.

I have been looking forward to a world where I shall get compensation for my cross:

But I have never thought of my cross as itself a present glory.

Teach me the glory of my cross:

Teach me the value of my thorn.

Shew me that I have climbed to Thee by the path of pain.

Shew me that my tears have made my rainbow."

— Anonymous.

CHAPTER 1

EVEN NOW ... I NEED ... A SAVIOR!

Sometimes profound thoughts can come from the darkest hearts!

It was the dark heart of the publican,
    Praying for mercy,
        Whose heart found light,
            Instead of the "luminous" Pharisee.

It was the one filthy sheep
    (The woman at the well)
Whose black heart cried for the worship of God –
    Not the ninety-nine righteous in the town!

Today there is little difference! It is the desperate heart which trembles at the blackness which possesses it and yearns for the Glory and Light of God to enter it ...

It is the desperate heart that stirs the Father's compassions –
    Not the intellect and expositors
Who no longer comprehend the magnitude of the power of our Savior
    But somehow feel that they,
        By some work and discipline of their own,
            Have made them what they are today.

The blackness and rot that the Savior mightily keeps from them no longer causes them to tremble at sin's awesome destruction or rejoice at the Redeemer's effective provision!

I don't need truth ...
    I need truth that can set me free!

I don't need suggestions, instructions, and demands ...
    I need a Savior!

Even Now ...

I don't need the ignorant unsympathetic sighs of disgust from the morally whole
　... I need the unimaginable incomprehensible mercy of God!

I don't need to hide scripture memorization in my mind ...
　I need Jesus in my heart!

I can't try hard enough, work long enough, or sorrow deep enough ...
　I need the limitless, generous, loving power of the Holy Spirit!

I can't tame, change, or clean my flesh – it must die!
　But death is not the goal ...
I need the Life of God and the communion of my Father!

Please, don't tell me to be stronger!
　All my power is utter contempt.

Don't tell me how you did it ...
　How strong you are ...
　　How much you delight in your holiness ...

I need to rejoice in the Holiness of another.
　I need a Redeemer – a Savior,
　　Who will do for me what I cannot do for myself!

Counsel me,
　But when you are done –
　　Be sure to know that I'm not one wit stronger.
I am only now more responsible and knowledgeable
　Regarding the crimes my flesh would run to.

So counsel me,
　But now I'm only educated...
　　Not changed!

Even Now ...

So counsel me,
    But when you're done,
        Pray for the keeping of God ...
For the Savior of all men to be:
    My portion,
        My deliverer,
            And my life-giver!

I need a Savior, a ruler to possess me.
    A Sovereign, to whom my whole will must submit!

And I need a Father!
    So that I'm not a subject to a tyrant,
        But the liberated joyful thankful son of the King!

I need to love and be loved!
    Not by any
        But by the great hand that has been offended
And whose heart has sent forth:
    Mercy instead of judgment,
        Kindness instead of revenge,
            Jesus instead of angels!

Dearest Heavenly Father,
    I have trusted in your Lovingkindness ...
        That Lovingkindness which has loved me,
            With an everlasting love,
                Which forgives,
                    Which cleanses,
                        And will never tire of me!

Father, I lean hard and heavy on you!
    I rest not, lean not, nor have confidence in my:
        Vows,
            Efforts,
                Or promises!

Even Now ...

Upon you alone, oh blessed Father, I place all hope.
  I lean with rest upon the faithfulness of your great Heart.
    I rejoice in the shadow of your wings!

At so great a salvation,
  I bow my head and humbly thank you
    For the Savior I so desperately needed ...
      And you so graciously provided!

Now unto you ...
  My Savior, who is able to keep me from falling.
Who alone is able to present me faultless
  Before the presence of His Glory with exceeding *joy*,
To the only wise God our Savior,
  Be glory and majesty,
    Dominion and power,
      Both now and ever.
                                             Amen!

CHAPTER 2

EVEN NOW ... IN THE NAME OF GOD

God's Secret Purpose

> Whatever the enemy of our souls can do to instill doubt about the real purpose of the Father of our souls, he will certainly try to do. "Hath God said?" was his question to Eve, and she trusted him, the enemy, and doubted God. Each time the suspicion arises that God is really "out to get us," that He is bent on making us miserable or thwarting any good we might seek, we are calling Him a liar. His secret purpose has been revealed to us, and it is to bring us finally, not to ruin, but to glory. That is precisely what the Bible tells us: "His secret purpose framed from the very beginning [is] to bring us to our full glory" (1 Cor. 2:7).
>
> I know of no more steadying hope on which to focus my mind when circumstances tempt me to wonder why God doesn't "do something." He is always doing something – the very best thing, the thing we ourselves would certainly choose if we knew the end from the beginning. He is at work to bring us to our full glory.
>
> — Elisabeth Elliot

My Vow,
Whatsoever Thou sayest unto me, by Thy grace I will do it.
My Constraint,
Thy love, O Christ, my Lord.
My Confidence,
Thou are able to keep that which I have committed unto Thee.
My Joy,
To do Thy will, O God.
My Discipline,
That which I would not choose, but which Thy love appoints.
My Prayer,
Conform my will to Thine.
My Motto,
Love to live: Live to love.
My Portion,
The Lord is the portion of mine inheritance

Even Now ...

Teach us, good Lord, to serve Thee more faithfully; to give and not to count the cost; to fight and not to heed the wounds; to toil and not seek for rest; to labour and not to ask for any reward, save that of knowing that we do Thy will, O Lord our God.
—Amy Carmichael

Psalm 20 expresses a common situation in which we find ourselves most often — in trouble!

The LORD hear thee in the day of trouble; the name of the God of Jacob defend thee; Send thee help from the sanctuary, and strengthen thee out of Zion; Remember all thy offerings, and accept thy burnt sacrifice; Selah. Grant thee according to thine own heart, and fulfill all thy counsel.

> We will rejoice in thy salvation, and in the name of our God we will set up *our* banners: the LORD fulfill all thy petitions. Now know I that the LORD saveth his anointed; he will hear him from his holy heaven with the saving strength of his right hand. Some *trust* in chariots, and some in horses: but we will remember the name of the LORD our God. They are brought down and fallen: but we are risen, and stand upright. Save, LORD: let the king hear us when we call (Psalm 20: 1-9).

The Lord is jealous for His name. Jeremiah, knowing the integrity God has for His name cries,

> O LORD, though our iniquities testify against us, do thou *it* for thy name's sake: for our backslidings are many; we have sinned against thee. O the hope of Israel, the saviour thereof in time of trouble, why shouldest thou be as a stranger in

the land, and as a wayfaring man *that* turneth aside to tarry for a night? Why shouldest thou be as a man astonied, as a mighty man *that* cannot save? yet thou, O LORD, *art* in the midst of us, and we are called by thy name; leave us not (Jeremiah 14:7 – 9).

When a man can position and entwine himself with God so that what becomes of him affects the glory of God's name, then that man is in a blessed state! With such sound confidence, as our previous scriptures show, that man who is tied to the name of God can call upon God for the forgiveness of his iniquities, for deliverance from his enemies, and for a defense from the weapons launched against him. For His name's sake, this man will see God unleash His unlimited arsenal of strength and power on his behalf. God will move heaven and earth; God will arise and the enemies will be scattered. Every trace of sin will be banished for that man who is looking to God!

That is wonderful! God is working for His name's sake, not because man has made himself worthy. Jeremiah admitted to sin among the people. They did not deserve help or benevolence. Yet they were able to cry for mercy from the hand of God, not because of intrinsic merit on their part, but because of God's name, and they were the people of His name! They expected forgiveness because God said His name was the Savior of Israel. So Israel called upon that name, "O the hope of Israel, the saviour thereof in time of trouble…" (Jeremiah 14:8).

I am thankful that God is not looking down saying, "OK, I saw how much you fasted last week. I saw those gigantic steps you took in Bible College. Because you have made yourself righteous and clean I am going to forgive your sins." I am glad that God has not committed His delivering power to those who seem so valuable and mighty. But for His name's sake God will show Himself strong even to the weak and poor.

It is true that a man has great confidence in the saving power of God in times of trouble when he has lived to honor and glorify God. As in Psalm 20, the faithful man can appeal to God to help him because he has sought God. But notice his appeal; I have brought my offerings to you. I have sacrificed to you. What is the Psalmist saying? He is confessing his need for God. He agrees with God that he is a weak man who can do nothing apart from God. He knows that he does not deserve help; therefore he has been faithful to sacrifice and offer his life to God in absolute humility and trust.

I rejoice and magnify my saving God, who through the blood of Jesus, is able to forgive my sins, deliver me from oppression, and rescue me from peril – all for the glory of His name!

THE NAME OF GOD AND THE DAY OF BATTLE

There is danger in this world. Trouble is everywhere. Men's hearts fail for fear. Disaster is all about. Terrorism has changed the lives of people all over the world. Economies are teetering on weak government subsidies. At any moment your world could collapse and come crashing down: your health could fail, your job could be terminated, and your spouse could leave.

However, if we have taken refuge in the name of God then there is a special favor that God extends. We need a place to run, a place of safety – a refuge. Today people are frantically running around seeking relief from their troubles. Therapists have never been busier. Most people have become addicted to prescription drugs because they are manic depressive and emotionally unstable. Bars are filled with the hollow laughter of people trying to drink their sorrows away. Religion has always been considered as a means of relief from the guilt of sin. However, none of these are valid solutions, but actually lead to an increase of the trouble from which people seek relief. In the church many are running to man, preachers, churches, and self-help programs yet they are as perplexed as the drunks in the bars.

So is there a place of relief? Is there a sound and reliable refuge? Yes! The name of the Lord is a strong tower, the righteous run into it and they are safe!

> We will rejoice in thy salvation, and in the name of our God we will set up *our* banners: the LORD fulfill all thy petitions (Psalm 20:5).

We will rejoice in your salvation. In the name of our God we will set up our banners. Banners were the flags with which armies marched forth into war; representing the kingdom the soldiers were joined to. Those flags (banners) represented something that was to strike fear in the enemy. The flag spoke. It was telling every aggressor that the entire power of the kingdom is behind us as we go to war. David is saying that when we go to war we will set up our banners in the name of God.

When did David set up his banners and rejoice? Was it after the battle? No! The battle is still to come. The enemy is out there and means to do us great harm. But in the name of God, David went to battle rejoicing in God's salvation. As the stage was being set for battle, David was setting up his banners. All over the place the flags were saying, "The name of my God is Strong Tower. The name of my God is Deliverer. The name of my God is Savior. The name of my God is Fortress. The name of my God is Sun and Shield!"

HOW DOES THIS APPLY TO YOUR BATTLES TODAY

Now, I want to show how this relates to you today. Jesus is the author and finisher of your faith. God begins your faith. God will finish your faith. Jesus is at work building your faith. Everything is done in your life to build your faith. If you're confused today, not knowing what is happening in your life, wondering where God is and what is going on, I can give you one simple answer. Jesus is building your faith. It may not look like it. It may not feel like it. But if you will remain faithful then this moment in your life will produce a greater faith.

And if God is building your faith then what is the outcome God intends for your life? I can promise you the outcome is not destruction. The outcome is not defeat, though God could be bringing your flesh to an end. God could be using the opportunity to humble you, but the outcome of God for your life is not destruction. God will not allow you to be defeated by the enemy if you are trusting in His grace. He will cause you to face things where you have to overcome, and for His name's sake you most certainly will overcome!

The trouble that you are in may cause you to cry out, "God what are you doing? God this is not comfortable. God I cannot see any good in this." God could respond, "I am answering your prayers! You wanted to be more like Jesus; this is the road! I am answering your prayers; you asked for strong faith, I am making it strong." It is through the circumstances and experience of life that your faith will be built.

SO GOD ALLOWS TRIALS FOR THOSE HE LOVES

The Psalmist asked, "Why is it that the wicked prosper?" It appears that the wicked get away with every awful thing they do. They even blaspheme God without any apparent consequence. It was not until the Psalmist went into the house of God that he understood their end and saw what was to become of them.

Do we not wonder about these things? Have you never questioned, "Have I washed my hands in vain?" All around you witness people who do not love God, who "seem" to be more contented than believers. Have you not asked, "Why is it that those that are in the will of God, empowered and anointed by God, face such opposition against their life? And why is it that those who neglect God, who are frivolous with the things of God, seem to encounter few problems and difficulties in life?"

Now we know the answer. The Bible tells us Satan is a very real enemy. The more serious you are about Jesus the more aggressively Satan will attack you; he will oppose your every step.

But oh how we wrestle and cry, "But God, you are God! If you would just knock him out then think of what we could accomplish for you. If you would just deal with Satan, we would not have to. Then we could devote ourselves to your desires! Here I am trying to do your will. Satan is hindering me – so deal with him God!" But God allows Satan to be Satan. And in all of Satan's schemes and aggressions God will work it for His own glory and build our faith.

This is portrayed in the godly king Jehoshaphat. He loves the Lord. After a time when the kings of Israel were rotten here is one that truly loves God. And wouldn't you know it; armies come seeking to destroy him. This really doesn't make sense. I could understand

God allowing this if the king was wicked. But this is a good king. I would expect God to shower him with blessings. I would expect God to help him. Never would I imagine that God would allow an army to come against him. However, it was the will of God that Jehoshaphat face opposition.

Jehoshaphat responds to this opposition with faith; he seeks God. This is the first thing he does. He does not turn to his military. He does not turn to his generals. He does not try to count the people. He just falls before God. That's the kind of heart and faith this man has as he cries to God, "An army has come against us; we need you God, we need your help."

> Behold, *I say, how* they reward us, to come to cast us out of thy possession, which thou hast given us to inherit. O our God, wilt thou not judge them? for we have no might against this great company that cometh against us; neither know we what to do: but our eyes *are* upon thee (2 Chronicles 20:11 – 12).

Jehoshaphat would not fit in with the positive faith movement. He tells God we have no might ... we do not know what to do. He is completely honest before God as he says that this army is stronger than we are. We cannot beat them. We need your help. Be honest before God. Let Him know you are hurting ... scared ... confused ... weak. You can confess to God the fact that you are facing things you cannot defeat. But also confess, "God, if you will help me I can win! I need your help."

If you don't know anything else in life, if you face a problem in which you do not know what to do, then all you need to do is this – look to God! Tell the Lord, "My eyes are upon you!" The moment you take your eyes off God you are defeated.

"And all Judah stood before the Lord, with their little ones, their wives, and their children." When we read a story that occurred thousands of years ago it is hard to understand the severity of the situation. Here is Jehoshaphat standing before God with the children of Israel!

Even Now ...

With their wives, babies, and children at their side, they cry out to God, "An army has come against us. These little children are about to die. We are going to be killed ... slaughtered, but our eyes are upon you! I do not know what to do. I do not have the might to conquer them. God, we are hopeless without you. Our babies are going to die. Our children will become slaves. Our wives are going to be raped. God, this is a severe situation. We are called by your name, arise and help us!"

Our problems are probably a little less severe than Jehoshaphat's, but still they are more than we can handle. So we fearfully cry, "God I don't have the finances to meet the needs in my home. I do not have the finances to pay my bills. I do not have the finances to feed my children. I do not know what I'm going to do. God I am so tired ... I am fainting. I have no more strength or desire. I want to quit, but I'm looking to you; this is all I know to do. I need you to help me. God I need you to do something!" That's real life!

Perhaps you are sick and the doctors have exhausted their efforts to cure you. Now that your days are numbered ... and all human help has vanished, look to God. Cry out to God, "For your name's sake help me. You said you are Jehovah Rapha. I believe you are my healer." Don't just lift up your banner when the trouble is over. Lift it up now! Don't just sing the praises of God when the doctors declare you are healed. Rejoice now! Triumphantly declare that in life or death my lips shall praise the Lord! When the enemy is breathing down your neck and it seems he holds your family in the bonds of wickedness, lift up your banner in the name of God. Shout to that devil, "For His name's sake God will deliver me. My God is Savior, and He will save my loved ones from your wicked grasp!"

A song we used to sing goes something like this,

God is too wise to be mistaken,
God is too good to be unkind.
  So when you don't understand,
     When you can't see His plan
     When you can't trace His hand
  Trust His heart.

CHAPTER 3

EVEN NOW... WHEN I NEED A MIRACLE

Lord, I am no longer my own, but Yours.
Put me to what You will,
    Rank me with whom You will.
Let me be employed by You
    Or laid aside for you,
Exalted for You
    Or brought low by You.
Let me have all things,
    Let me have nothing,
I freely and heartily yield all things to Your pleasure and disposal.
    And now, O glorious and blessed God,
      Father, Son, and Holy Spirit,
You are mine and I am Yours.
    So be it.
Amen.

                      — John Wesley

My Father, there are reasons why I could feel downcast.
When I think about some parts of my life it's hard to pray –
    Even harder to worship in freedom….
        … Relationships that are difficult …
            … Dreams and goals that are crumbling …
                … Old hurts that wound me over and over. …
Some parts of me feel cold and wordless. …
    Is the problem that I've buried some things deep inside?
Are you patiently calling –
    Through days and months –
        For me to open up to you at some deeper level?
            Today, Father, I trust you to go deeper.
                      — Amy Carmichael

Think how foolish Jehoshaphat appeared; falling before a God he could not see. Reaching out to a God he could not touch.

Surely people must have thought, "Wake up man! This is a battle. This is war. Tomorrow they will be killing you and raping your wives! Mount your troops. Enlist your soldiers. Gather the generals for briefings. Man the stations and fight for your lives! Better to fight and die than not to fight and be taken as slaves."

That is the counsel of most people.

But Jehoshaphat knew God. Though he appeared foolish to some, he knew he was not a fool to seek God. Only the fool would face this situation apart from God. He knew that God would deliver. God would fight for them.

Now this is truth that you must believe. If you are walking in God's will and trusting in God, He will never allow anything to destroy you. You may think something is going to kill you. You may even want to die, but you will not! God wants your faith to grow! And how does your faith grow? By letting God deliver you! Why do you trust God? Because He proves trustworthy! He is not going to let you be ashamed! He is showing you to trust Him. He is showing you His way.

In Jehoshaphat's situation, before they even face this great enemy, Israel is falling before God and worshipping Him! There was a roar in the camp! It was the sound of victory. And the battle had not even begun. How is that possible? It is possible because God promised to fight for them and they believed Him! And the Levites roared with praise to God!

I imagine this invading army heard that roar of praise and became very concerned and fearful. Sometimes God is waiting for your shout of praise before He brings your deliverance! Perhaps your trials have not ended because you have not lifted your voice in praise to God. Instead you are filled with despair ... defeat ... and skepticism. You know God can but you do not believe God will! Your heart is not shouting. Your heart is not rejoicing. Praise is not coming forth. Instead there is skepticism that says, "I will believe it when I see it. I will praise after the battle but not before!"

Anyone can praise after the battle but it takes faith to praise before the battle starts! So what happened to Jehoshaphat? The Lord was faithful to Jehoshaphat and delivered him from his enemy. And Jehoshaphat had peace, for God gave him rest round about.

God brought rest into his life and kingdom because his heart was fixed upon God. Jehoshaphat had rest because he knew God, not because he was without enemies! Jehoshaphat had rest because he praised God in good times and bad and could rejoice in His salvation before his battles even started.

This ability to praise is the assurance that God is my deliverer and I will not be overcome. When a person has lost the note of praise he has already lost the battle he must still face. The life God gives is joyful. What can disturb the peace of those whose eyes are fixed upon God even though there are disturbances all around?

However, I know what some are thinking. We have all thought it. We have thought it because we have all had to deal with it. You know what I am referring to! Those times in our life when we really trusted God, but He didn't answer; the help did not come!

So some of you are reading this saying, "I want to trust God but it is hard. I have trusted before and it did not appear that God was faithful to me. Why did He not come to my aid?" If you keep reading, I will answer that question!

WHEN GOD DOESN'T SEEM FAITHFUL

> Now Jesus loved Martha, and her sister, and Lazarus. ⁶When he had heard therefore that he was sick, he abode two days still in the same place where he was ... Then Martha, as soon

as she heard that Jesus was coming, went and met him ... (John 11:5 – 6, 20).

That is a strange love. Maybe there is a mistake here. Perhaps it should read, "Now Jesus loved Martha, Mary, and Lazarus so when he heard that Lazarus was sick he arose immediately and went to him." But that is not what Jesus did and there is no mistake here. Jesus loved them! But like Martha and Mary, what do we do when it seems God has forsaken us? Is this not the biggest test of our faith – still to believe, even when it appears that God has failed us? Oh the absence of God in our time of need! Why does this happen? Have you experienced this? Have you ever cried out, "God where are you? Why have you forsaken me?"

Jesus loved this family and He loves you. It was Jesus' love for Martha, Mary and Lazarus that caused Him to delay His coming until Lazarus was dead four days. It was then, when Lazarus was dead, that Jesus rose up explaining to his disciples that this family needed His help.

Martha met Jesus as He was approaching the town. She was confused. Make no doubt about it; she was confused. She did not understand. She wondered at what she considered to be the negligence of Jesus. She poured it all out at Jesus' feet; she laid it out before God, "If you had been here ... I feel let down ... I do not understand. You love us. We love you. We are not strangers. You were not here when we needed you. Jesus, if you had been here!" Now this is what is going on in her heart. But do not forget for one moment that this is a woman of faith, so read her words.

> Then said Martha unto Jesus, Lord, if thou hadst been here, my brother had not died. But I know, that even now, whatsoever thou wilt ask of God, God will give *it* thee (John 11:21 – 22).

How wonderful is her faith as she says, "... I know, that even now, whatsoever thou wilt ask of God, God will give *it* thee." The necessity of this faith in the midst of our battles could never be overstated. Can you say in the midst of whatever it is you're dealing with, "Even now ... Even now I know ...." Do you really know, or do you hope and wonder and think and want it to be? Or as Martha, do you know?

I know your problem is great, but look at Martha. Her brother was in a grave. Take your biggest trial; bring it to the feet of Jesus and look up to him saying, "Even now, Lord, I know that whatever you ask, your Father will give it to you."

YOUR STORY MAY BE DIFFERENT BUT YOUR NEED IS THE SAME

Though Martha's story is different from Jehoshaphat's, their faith in God is the same! Though Martha was not fighting an army and Jehoshaphat was not standing at the grave of a brother – they both faced situations where God was needed. Bring your needs to Jesus; even now He can help you! Have you fallen in great sin? Does it seem that your rebellion has destroyed your future? I tell you that "Even Now" the mighty Savior can help you!

He is the God of hope!

    He is the God of all comfort!

        He is the Savior.

            He is the God of the impossible!

                He is the resurrection and the life!

He is the God who shouts, "Is there anything too hard for me?"

    He is the God of the breakthrough!

        He is the God of victory!

He is the God who created everything out of nothing and can create a new life for you. He wants you to come ... in the midst of anything ... when life is most difficult and say, "Even Now, God."

THIS IS THE STORY OF THE BIBLE

This is the story of the Bible! Adam and Eve have rebelled against God. Death has entered. Judgment is here, and judgment is coming. Adam now dreaded the God he once walked with. God had told him that in the day that he ate of this fruit he would die, yet in the midst of this doom the "Even Now" God shows up. He comes to the fallen man with animal skins and a promise. "Even Now," in the midst of sin and rebellion, a chosen woman shall have a Son who will save them and crush the serpent's head!

I think about Moses, spared in his birth because of the call of God upon his life. He is brought up as a prince. Knowing he has something to do with the deliverance of Israel, he took matters into his own hands. He murdered an Egyptian. He was rejected by Israel and fled for his life. In a moment Moses was demoted from prince of the most powerful nation on earth, to an obscure shepherd somewhere in the desert. For forty years he had no contact with God. But one day he encountered a fiery bush that was not consumed by the fire. God spoke to him. After forty years, "Even Now," God had come to use his life!

Joseph is rejected by his family. With poisonous hate they sold him into slavery. From there he was condemned to prison. Why was this happening to him? He was supposed to be a ruler. His brothers were supposed to bow at his feet. His father was supposed to honor him. Was Joseph wrong? Did he make a mistake about his dreams, or has he just made them up? Thirteen years passed; Joseph was forgotten in prison. But "Even Now", Joseph, God can take you from prison to the throne – in a day, "Even Now!"

David ... psalmist ... worshiper of God, committed adultery. But his sins did not stop there. In a massive effort to cover his crime, he performed a campaign of lies, betrayal, and conspiracy. He even murdered the woman's husband in an effort to conceal his wicked deeds. But David could not hide. He was exposed by God before the

Even Now ...

entire nation. Yet after all of David's schemes the "Even Now" God says, "You are a man after my own heart."

What am I telling you? That many of you think your fate is sealed. You have given up. There is no shout of praise, no roar of rejoicing. However, God wants to say to you, "Even Now, in the midst of 'whatever,' I am God! If, as Martha, you can believe me, then Even Now I will create something beautiful out of this mess!"

Japheth was an illegitimate embarrassment to his family, but "Even Now" God raised him up to be a judge in Israel.

Samson was a lustful, sex-crazed, self-indulgent, careless man. He had broken his covenant with God. He had lost his eyes and become the play toy of his enemies. He was horrible. He was wicked. But on the day of his death he set his heart back upon God. "Even Now," Samson, because you look to the Lord, God will give you strength. You will have more glory in your death than you did in all your living – "Even Now!" Even Now! What hope God gives us!

Sara's womb was dead. She was in her nineties. Abraham was approaching one hundred years old! But "Even Now," in this helplessness God could produce a baby.

The Shunamite woman's son was dead. She laid the corpse on the prophet's bed. Past all of the people, she ran until she got to the prophet of God. Though her boy was dead, she knew that "Even Now" God could raise him up!

Rejecting the call of God, Jonah ran from the Lord. He was in deep trouble. Death had swallowed him. But "Even Now" from the belly of hell he cried, and God heard him and forgave him!

Habakkuk said, "Though the fig tree does not blossom, though there are no cattle in the stalls, and no grain to grind from the field, [Even Now] I will rejoice in the Lord; I will exult in the God of my salvation. [Even Now] the Lord is my Strength and my invincible army: He makes my feet like hinds' feet and will make me to walk upon my high places!"

The widow had one cake left to eat with her son, and then they would die of the famine. But "Even Now" if she gave that cake to the prophet, God would sustain her through the famine.

Elijah was depressed wanting to die. Imagine the great prophet sitting in a cave begging God to take his life. Instead, God comes into the midst of that depression assuring Elijah that "Even Now" I have a greater work for you to do!

Naaman was dying with leprosy. He does not understand how dipping in the Jordan seven times could cure his disease. He balked at the prophet's instructions. But his little servant having so much wisdom and faith, said that if God had asked you to do something difficult, you would have done it. So "Even Now" he dipped. Six times he went down into Jordan. Six times he came up infested with leprosy. But "Even Now" he went down into Jordan the seventh time and out he came, healed and clean!

So many have tried but keep falling short. But now is the time ... "Even Now" ... right now!

Elisha and his servant were surrounded by the Syrian army but "Even Now" the armies of God were with them.

The woman at the well was going into her fifth marriage. She was a hopeless basket case wanting to know who God was, with no one to tell her. But "Even Now" God came to her when she least expected it and satisfied her life.

Paul was persecuting Christians, arresting them, sending them to prison and their death. When Jesus met him on the road to Damascus it was an "Even Now" moment. Jesus seized this terrorist and converted him into the mighty apostle!

Five thousand hungry men had been following Jesus for days. The disciples were commanded to feed them but could find no possible way. However, Andrew found a boy with some bread and fish. Not knowing how this small provision would help so many, he did know that if he could get it to Jesus that "Even Now" Jesus could make it work.

Martha looked up into the face of Jesus; her brother had been in the grave for four days. This was a hopeless situation. She was hurting. She did not understand, "If you had been here ... but 'Even Now' ...."

Do you have that faith? Even if it is sin that has destroyed your hopes for a future or if it is a broken home ... or sexual molestation ... or the death of someone very special to you – "Even Now" He is a Savior.

Even Now …

It does not matter how impure your heart may really be – "Even Now" He is the purifier of hearts. It doesn't matter how bad the sickness – "Even Now" He is the healer. "Even Now" He is the deliverer … "Even Now" He is God!

CHAPTER 4

EVEN NOW ... WHAT DEFINES YOU?

"See in this" –
    This provoking, this rebuke that should not have been –
        "A chance to die."
To self, and the pride that comes from defending self.
"See in anything" –
    Anything that rouses you to claim your "rights,"
        Or even to consider them at all –
            "A chance to die". ...
Welcome anything that calls you to your only true position:
    "I have been crucified with Christ ..." (Galatians 2:20).
A crucified life cannot be self-assertive.
    It cannot protect itself.
        It cannot be startled into resentful words.
The cup that is full of sweet water cannot spill bitter-tasting drops,
    However sharply it is knocked.

                — Amy Carmichael

No man is ever fully accepted until he has, first of all,
    Been utterly rejected.

                — Author unknown

Jesus loved Lazarus. However, when requested to come to the ailing Lazarus Jesus stayed where He was and did not attend to Lazarus. What kind of love is this? Failing to understand God's love when it appears He does not care for us causes many to forgo the incredible blessings God desires to bestow! God does love us and sometimes He does not answer us as we wish ... sometimes it appears He has neglected us. If we will continue to trust in His love we will see the glory of God.

Jesus allowed people He loved to suffer greatly. Lazarus did not die from old age or a sudden tragedy; he was sick. Jesus' love allowed Lazarus to suffer to such a point that eventually the sickness took his life. It was then, after Lazarus was dead for four days, that Jesus went to them - a little late it surely appears!

Jesus allowed a family He loved to mourn the death of their beloved brother for four days before He even showed up. Jesus did not even come to the funeral! He did not even come to console the mourners. He was not even there to comfort the family. Yet the Bible says He loved them.

Martha ran out to meet Jesus telling him that if He had been here Lazarus would not have died. Yet in the midst of this tragedy she says the most remarkable words, "Even Now whatever you ask your Father He will give you ...."

CAN YOUR FAITH ROLL STONES AWAY

Can you say, "Even Now, Lord whatever You will …?" As Martha, can you do more than say words; can you take the next step? Can you roll the stones away? Can you remove the self imposed barriers barring you from God's ordained destiny? What is it that has sealed your fate or robbed you of your dreams? Can you roll it away?

Jesus didn't roll the stone away; He commanded Martha to do it. Martha had to roll the stone away.

Many have watched their dreams go by, desires vanish, and hearts break; and the whole time God was there standing before them, waiting to hear them say, "Even Now Lord …!" Unlike Martha, too many focus on the perceived reality and say, "Oh no, not now Jesus. I can say the right thing, 'Even Now …' but when you tell me to roll the stone away something inside says, 'Not now Jesus! Not now. I don't know that I believe this.'"

DAVID COULD ROLL STONES AWAY

Few have displayed assurance in God more than David. Time and again he had things stripped from his life. He was hounded by armies, and even his own son sought his demise, but David had God. As a matter of fact, God was the only thing David had. Time and again David rolled his stones away. Throughout his life David fell on God and was broken into a very strong man.

> And whosoever shall fall on this stone shall be broken: but on whomsoever it shall fall, it will grind him to powder (Matthew 21:44).

Think about falling. There are no props. You are no longer hanging on. You are helpless and at the mercy of any who can save – for a moment you are finally free. Just before you fell, you thought you were in control. Now that you are falling you realize how slippery life can be. Now you suddenly have no control, nothing makes sense; nothing is working out for you. You pray, "I'm falling God.

I'm falling apart. God, you alone can help me ... you can save me ... you can catch me!" To fall upon this rock is to break every superficial string in life. It is to be free! To fall on this rock means you want everything cut, you will no longer allow your life to be pulled in a thousand different directions. You are tired of the superficial life you have been living. You are tired of simply reading the Bible, singing the songs, and going to the services; so you cry, "God, I cut it all off. I'm falling on you – give me reality!"

Something is gained in the falling – it is freedom! It is the freedom which comes by knowing I am not in control. The freedom that confesses I have never been in control, and the joyful confidence of resting in God who will not fail me. It is the freedom which lays hold of the truth that nothing can separate me from God, and nothing can separate God from me! But to have this freedom I must fall on this rock and that is hard to do.

Falling is just that — falling. Life is out of your control. There is uncertainty; how will you hit? How will you land? How will things turn out? It is those situations in life, like Martha with her dead brother, that make you doubt whether your life is in His hands. And the proof of God's love and faithfulness only appears at the conclusion of the trial, though in actuality His love and faithfulness were with you the whole time.

DAVID'S LIFE IS OUT OF CONTROL

In 2 Samuel, we read that David's home life was in disarray. Amnon, David's son, lusted for Tamar his half-sister. Pretending to be sick, Amnon requested that Tamar care for him. While Tamar was nursing his needs, Amnon raped her. Now Absalom, Tamar's brother and Amnon's half-brother, was frustrated that David took no disciplinary action against Amnon. Consumed with anger and rage, Absalom planned his sister's revenge.

After the passage of time, Absalom invited his brothers on a camping trip. While there, Absalom had given his men orders to take Amnon and kill him. Absalom, afraid to return home, fled to another country where he lived for some time. Absalom then orchestrated a very successful coup against the throne of his father David.

Wounded, angry, neglected, and disgusted with his father's injustice Absalom begins to rip the kingdom from David.

Absalom had the uncanny ability to steal the hearts of the people. He sat at the gate and seduced the people, "You know if my dad were a good king he would have people here caring for you. He would have people here giving you attention. Nobody is here to give you attention, except for me – Absalom; I am here for you. I care about you, and if you would make me king then I could care for you and see that you get the justice you deserve (author's paraphrase)."

The people would come and bow down to Absalom, kissing him as he would give them affection and attention while promising them wonderful things. He convinced Israel to follow him as their king. Now it was obvious that Absalom really didn't care about Israel. He wanted to destroy his father and he would use and abuse anyone to do it.

The Bible says, "... Absalom stole the hearts of the men of Israel" (2 Samuel 15:6). And affirms, "... the conspiracy was strong; for the people increased continually with Absalom" (2 Samuel 15:12).

WHO IS THIS DAVID THAT IS FALLING

There will be no greater opportunity to discover what David is truly about, what kind of man he really is than right here ... right now, in this moment of rejection and hopelessness. As king he can begin mass executions of all the rebels, including his son. Other kings have, they have massacred their entire family rather than lose their power. David controls the army. He could really show Israel how strong he is. He could put so much fear into the people that they would never again rebel against him. David could hit this insurrection with such an iron fist that all future desires for a coup would end in the minds of the trembling weak fools who would even think to mess with David. But this is not what he does. Instead David flees!

> And the king went forth, and all the people after him, and tarried in a place that was far off. And all his servants passed on beside him; and all the Cherethites, and all the Pelethites,

and all the Gittites, six hundred men which came after him from Gath, passed on before the king. Then said the king to Ittai the Gittite, Wherefore goest thou also with us? Return to thy place, and abide with the king: for thou *art* a stranger, and also an exile (2 Samuel 15:17 – 19).

This is an exodus. For all intent and purposes, David is falling. Every superficial string is being cut. Yesterday David was king ... David was in control. However, today, David's life is spiraling out of control; he may have lost everything.

It is humiliating for the King to have to leave his capital city. Why does David do this? Why not smash the uprising? Now come on, think for a moment. David had four hundred mighty men who alone could have devastated this coup. Why not fight or die?

This is not a proud moment. It is not one of David's glory days; this is humiliating.

And David does not flee alone. The men following David, in a day of dishonor, are doing so because they believe in David. They love him. They are loyal. This is a large group of soldiers who will follow David anywhere and do anything required of them. Just consider the response of Ittai,

Then said the king to Ittai the Gittite, Wherefore goest thou also with us? return to thy place, and abide with the king: for thou *art* a stranger, and also an exile. Whereas thou camest *but* yesterday, should I this day make thee go up and down with us? seeing I go whither I may, return thou, and take back thy brethren: mercy and truth *be* with thee. And Ittai answered the king, and said, *As* the LORD liveth, and *as* my lord the king liveth, surely in what place my lord the king shall be, whether in death or life, even there also will thy servant be (2 Samuel 15:19 – 21).

You know what is interesting? What is interesting is who is not following David! He is leaving Jerusalem with six hundred Philistines, his mighty men and family. Where is Israel? Where are all the people who would be slaves if it were not for the heroics of

David? This is David, the man who had laid his life down for Israel's safety. His courage and sacrifice brought liberty to all of Israel. He fought back their oppressors. He took to the battlefields so that the Israelites could take to their homes and businesses! If it were not for David, they would all be slaves!

When I think about the people following David as compared to those who came hurling insults, I could only consider how fickle people are: One minute they are for you and the next they stand against you. One moment they are in the streets praising you, and the next they are in the crowd crying for your crucifixion. People will love you and applaud at your coronation. However, they can't wait for the day of your humiliation. And when your humiliation comes they will be obnoxiously happy.

But David is a wise man. It is worth noting that David never tries to recruit people to his side. He actually attempts to discourage those who are following him. He encourages them to stay in their homes telling them that he does not know what will happen or if he will ever return to Jerusalem. He makes it very clear that his life is in disarray and even assures them that God may be against him. He just does not know what is going on. Surely David realized this was no time to surround himself with suspicious men. This ingenious move by David, his act of discouraging many from following, sanctified a group around David who were completely loyal. If you have to persuade men to stand with you then you are only taking on traitors.

DON'T FIGHT – FALL

As David flees, one of King Saul's descendants follows David mocking and throwing stones saying, "Come out, come out, thou bloody man, and thou man of Belial: The LORD hath returned upon thee all the blood of the house of Saul, in whose stead thou hast reigned; and the LORD hath delivered the kingdom into the hand of Absalom thy son: and, behold, thou *art taken* in thy mischief, because thou *art* a bloody man" (2 Samuel 16:7 – 8).

Imagine that – calling David a devil! You can only surmise what David's mighty men must have been thinking. Surely they were chomping at the bits to destroy this man. As a matter of fact Abishai asked David for permission to decapitate the man saying, "Why should this dead dog curse my lord the king?" (2 Samuel 16:9)

However, falling upon God, David says, "So let him curse, because the LORD hath said unto him, Curse David. Who shall then say, Wherefore hast thou done so? And David said to Abishai, and to all his servants, Behold, my son, which came forth of my bowels, seeketh my life: how much more now *may this* Benjamite *do it*? let him alone, and let him curse; for the LORD hath bidden him. It may be that the LORD will look on mine affliction, and that the LORD will requite me good for his cursing this day" (2 Samuel 16:10 – 12).

FALLING IS HARD

The reality of falling is hard. This is not a game; it is for real as we cry, "How am I going to pay these bills? What will I do for a job?" I do not know how many times God has pulled this church away from me, and I have become terrified crying, "God what will I do? How will I survive? I can't do anything else!" We all fall. Each life must deal with its own crisis of terror!

David teaches me so much about falling on God. I love the silence and quiet of David's spirit as he is falling; there is no vengeance, no fight in the fighter! He just falls realizing confusing things are happening. He knows he failed to do things that should have been done. He knows he was not the father his children needed. He knows he allowed his daughter to be raped with no consequence and a son to be murdered. David knows that he never reached out to Absalom to help him deal with the raw wounds of hate in his heart.

David considers that he may be getting what he deserves, realizing that he has not been the most faithful man. He considers the fact that God may be taking the throne from him! I thank God the Bible is so honest and transparent with its greatest examples of the faith! David the great worshipper of God does not know what is going on!

David did not fight the fact that events in his life were spinning out of control. He humbled himself before God and trusted the Lord to care for him. He would not even allow the Ark of the Covenant to accompany him. Yet most people would manipulate and connive in a futile attempt to regain control and order of their circumstances. However, this effort to end their dilemma typically aggravates the problem even more. David has taught me two profound lessons about falling and having faith for "Even Now."

FIRST, DO NOT LOSE WHAT IS MOST IMPORTANT

David realized there was one thing he could not afford to lose, and it was not his throne! Some things are not as important as people make them out to be. For David the throne was not all-important – he could leave it. He did not think it was a thing to be grasping after. This spirit is the Spirit of Christ revealed in Philippians 2:5-9:

> Let this mind be in you, which was also in Christ Jesus: Who, being in the form of God, thought it not robbery to be equal with God: But made himself of no reputation, and took upon him the form of a servant, and was made in the likeness of men: And being found in fashion as a man, he humbled himself, and became obedient unto death, even the death of the cross. Wherefore God also hath highly exalted him, and given him a name which is above every name ...

Surely David remembered when another man was king in Israel. While Saul was king, many believed David should have the throne; however, David refused to take the matter into his own hands. If God wanted David to be king, then let God do it! He saw the jealousy Saul had for the throne. He saw how it destroyed his life. David watched the terror in Saul; so consumed was Saul to keep the throne at all cost he eventually lost God!

David was more afraid of losing God than of losing the throne. The throne was not that important to him – he could leave it; he could walk away from it. There are greater things in life.

SECOND, WHAT DEFINES YOU

I glean from this episode in David's life the question, "What defines you?" Personally I had to know – what defines me? Is it a pulpit that defines me? If God were to take me out of the pulpit what would I become? If God removed me from my position what do I become? If people sang the praises of another and my popularity decreased would I rejoice in their anointing, or like Saul, would I be enraged in jealousy? So many are defined by what they do. They are given the accolades of being a "man of God" because of what they do. But take their office away and what are they left with? Maybe they are not what they used to be; the feelings of zeal, hunger, passion, and desire for God are gone. Now all they love is what they do. They are passionate about what they do. They love the position, the recognition, the power – they have become Sauls! And like Saul they will tear the church down if anyone tries to take their position away. Unlike David who just simply walked out and went to a desert place and worshipped God, some have become obsessed with their office, obsessed with their position, and believe that it's something worth fighting for and grasping after; dare even God to take this from them!

But I wonder what would happen if He did? What would happen if God took your Sunday school class from you? What if some missionaries were called off the field and their position was taken from them? Would they be any different, or would they continue to be zealous for the Lord? Would they continue to be fervent?

We are so defined by offices but David wasn't. David is different! David did not grasp after the position and power. He took refuge in the only thing that was sure, "[And] David went up ... *mount* Olivet, and wept as he went up, and had his head covered, and he went barefoot ... *when* David was come to the top *of the mount* ... he worshipped God ... (2 Samuel 15:30 – 32).

So here is the answer to my question, "Take the throne from David and what are you left with?" And the answer is – a worshipper! Take David's position away and what does he become? What he was before he was ever king, a man of God ... a worshipper; a lover of God who could demonstrate his all-consuming delight and passion,

"One *thing* have I desired of the LORD, that will I seek after; that I may dwell in the house of the LORD all the days of my life, to behold the beauty of the LORD, and to enquire in his temple" (Psalm 27:4). That is the David you are left with.

Remove it all from David and you are left with the same man you started with when as a boy he lay under the stars considering the majesty of God. Now he has been involved in all of the trappings of success: the throne, the kingdom, and all the glory that comes with them. Yet in the midst of it all, he never lost his God, he never lost his heart! Take his throne away. Take his position away. Humiliate him. And what does he do? He falls on his face and worships God! David was not defined by a throne! David was not defined by a kingdom!

So what about you? Are you defined by a Sunday school class? Are you defined as a preacher in a pulpit? Are you defined as a missionary? How do you tell? Take it away, and will you be found in the prayer meetings hungry for God, seeking after God? Take your pulpit away, and will you be found in passionate worship? Take your position and ministry away, and will you still study the Word, hungry to learn, yearning to be closer to God?

Do not allow any thing ever to happen in your life where Jesus is no longer the most important thing to you. Never judge the fact that Jesus is important to you by what you do or what men say of you. Rather examine your heart and discern the fire and hunger you have for Jesus Christ!

Oh, God, I want to fall, I want to fall on this rock. I want all the superficial strings to be cut! I want to fall. I don't want to be defined by the trappings of success in the eyes of man. Oh God save me from being lost in what I do that I am no longer defined by who I am – a man after God's own heart. Save me from the faithfulness to a duty that causes me to lose the fervency of worship and the longings for your presence.

God will test people by taking things away. Oh it is coming! You had better believe it.

Even Now ...

Just ask Abraham when God required Isaac.

Just ask Jonah when God required the gourd.

And just ask David as God required the throne!

In this episode of David's life surely God was asking, "Is it true, son? Is my loving kindness better than life? Let's see son! Let's see if it is. Am I more important to you than anything? David, is it true that there is only one thing that you seek, one thing that you desire? Well let's see; I am going to take it from you: the fame, the money, the popularity, the power. Do not fight for it! Just fall! Fall to your freedom. Fall to your rest. Fall upon me! I will not allow you to be crushed; I will catch you. I will restore you!"

Falling is so hard. Sometimes I think God makes you cut the last string! Or He makes you roll the stone away. Certainly this is the hard part. It is easy to say the right thing but when God requires me to roll the stone away or to cut the last string that I may fall, can I do it? If I cut this string, I am falling. This string keeps me in this place. But I do not like this place. Sure, everything is good: the money is good, the position is good, the recognition is good, the preaching is good, the pulpit is good. Oh, but God, those days when it was just you and I under the stars and walking together, life was simple; I hungered for you, I longed for you – Oh God I still want to be that man no matter what!

Chapter 5

EVEN NOW ... WHEN I DON'T FEEL LIKE IT

If you would live in victory over the circumstances,
    Great and small, that come to you each day …
… And if you want God's life and power to well up from the depths of your being
    … Then you must refuse to be dominated by the seen and the felt.
You say: "I could climb mountains if God asked me to. That would be a joy!
    But here I stand, on this dreary seashore of my life,
        looking over this dreary backwash bay and a drearier shoreline –
            and beyond that, inland, no mountains.
    Nothing invigorating, or inspiring.
        Nothing hard enough to inspire anyone. …"
The whole of my life is like that these days – not hard, just dull.
I would have chosen challenging over dull.
A challenge that would make me want to achieve at any cost.
It's this useless feeling that's so devastating.

— Amy Carmichael

Be not deceived; God is not mocked: for whatsoever a man soweth, that shall he also reap. For he that soweth to his flesh shall of the flesh reap corruption; but he that soweth to the Spirit shall of the Spirit reap life everlasting. And let us not be weary in well doing: for in due season we shall reap, if we faint not (Galatians 6:7 – 9).

Though Satan is a worthy foe, the greatest devastation that strikes is the domination of my emotions: how I feel about things ... what I feel like doing ... how I feel like acting ... what I feel like believing. Whenever my feelings affect my thinking and faith I will want to quit life. In difficult times, my feelings will depress me and make me want to give up, discouraging me with gloomy thoughts and causing me to wonder why there is a point in trying anymore.

The paralysis of pain and gloomy emotions make us say, "I don't feel like being faithful today ... I'm hurting ... when things get better." But God declares, "They that sow in tears shall reap in joy. He that goeth forth and weepeth, bearing precious seed, shall doubtless come again with rejoicing, bringing his sheaves with him" (Psalm 126:5-6).

GOD WARNS – DO NOT LIVE BY YOUR FEELINGS

The act of sowing brings no more difficulty than reaping, both are very demanding jobs. Obviously the reason for tears is not because of the work. Sowing with tears and reaping with joy reveals there are other things going on.

The passage in Psalms refers to a time of great heartache, fatigue, and distress. It describes those moments in life when you are pressed in and feel as though you are being crushed and you don't want to "go on" anymore. Through this passage God is telling you to be productive even when you do not feel like it, even when your heart is broken.

Some people give up and throw in the towel. They quit life for the moment. According to the Psalm, there is a very sad outcome for those who quit living for tomorrow because of the pain of today – they will not reap! People who allow pain and suffering to prevent them from being productive will rarely see anything good transpire in their futures. Because some are unwilling to believe for the future and go forth sowing precious seed, they will instead allow their hurt feelings to rob them of all future joy! However, there are those who continue to live even though they have to cry to get through the day, but they live because they know things are going to change. They know times will get better because they are planting something good in this misery that will give them blessings later!

ANYBODY CAN GIVE UP — IT TAKES FAITH TO GO ON

Many people could allow their emotions or injustices to rule them and say, "I'm just too sad right now. My heart is too broken; I just can't go and sow this field today. I just can't go and plant these seeds. I'm heartbroken; I just don't feel like it today. Let somebody else do it."

If you live like that you won't be eating in the winter. If you don't sow your seeds in this pain there won't be food in the winter. So whether it is fun or not, whether you are happy or sad, whether you feel blessed or cursed – take your seeds and sow them. You will be glad you did when harvest time comes.

Your crops, your future, your destiny are not going to wait for you to get through crying! Your harvest is not going to wait till your problems go away. If you do not go forth, "Even Now," then the blessings you could have had may pass you *by*.

PAUL SOWED IN TEARS

The apostle Paul was often in weakness and feebleness. He was in death often, despairing for his life. He was frequently thrown into prison and was beaten so many times that he lost count. Five times he was whipped by the Jews. Three times he was beaten with rods. Once he was stoned. Three times he was shipwrecked at sea. For a night and a day he floated in the ocean. His journeys put him in constant danger: from rivers, robbers, Gentiles, and his own people. He faced dangers in the city, the wilderness, the sea, and the church. His labors were very demanding and hard, causing him sleepless nights. Often he went hungry and faced harsh conditions of cold and exposure, but he kept sowing! And look at the achievement, the accomplishments. What depth of ministry. What fullness of life. Paul is mightier today than when he was alive! And all of these blessings came because he refused to give in to the pain and heartache choosing rather to sow. He chose to live and not die! He did his duty and refused to let his feelings, emotions, and bad days keep him from doing what God had called him to do.

PREACH YOURSELF OUT OF THIS LOW PLACE

"Even Now," in our own lives, we have to take our future and sow it. We have to live for what will be and not what is! The times will change. Things will get better. Trials do end. Blessings will come. Victory is real! Preach to yourself, "If Paul and Silas could sing in prison then, by God, I can sing right now. If that widow could take her last cake and prepare it for the prophet then, in Jesus name, I can take what I feel is the last thing I have in my life and give it to God – and there will be a harvest! If Mary and Martha could walk to the tomb of their dead brother and command that stone to be rolled away, then by God I can rise up from this death and low place and see the glory of God as well."

There has to be an attitude ... a faith that moves you from where you are to where you need to be. Preach the truth to yourself, "I know that God will never leave me. He will not forsake me! God has plans for my life ... He has promised all things work together for good to those who love Him and I love Him! I do not know why all this is happening to me. I do not understand why all this heartache is occurring, but I know God has not forsaken me. God has a purpose and God will bring me forth!"

Even Now …

They say that as the body of the 83 year old Amy Carmichael lay upon her bed, the boys surrounded her lifeless body and sang praises to God for over thirty minutes!

Amy's was a full life, abundant with blessings and privileges that few have ever tasted. But it was not always easy. She wrote,

> Not relief from pain, not relief from the weariness that follows, not anything of that sort at all, is my chief need. Thou, O Lord my God, art my need – Thy courage, Thy patience, Thy fortitude. And very much I need a quickened gratitude for the countless helps given every day.

How did she learn to say that? She learned it by sowing in the hard times so there might be a future to reap! And what a future she did reap and will reap. Even today her life is changing the hearts of men and women around the world! By the time of her passing she had a family of thousands who called her the beloved Amma.

"Even Now" overcome this low place. Realize that you may have to suffer a little while. Hard times are normal. The world will not reward you. But in Christ you are an overcomer and in the end of the matter:

You will have your faith,

    You will have run your race,

        You will have fought a good fight,

            You will have WON!

TAKE AUTHORITY OVER YOURSELF IN JESUS NAME

Say to your tears, "I feel you. You make me want to quit life, but there is a field to be sown, dishes to be washed, a car to be fixed, sermons to be written."

I have to preach to myself, "These tears cannot determine my future." I must refuse to give in to my feelings as severe as they may be. Preach to yourself, "Tears! I know you will not stay forever. A harvest of blessing will be mine when you have long dried up!"

Tears are the result of things that have been or the fear of what could be. If you are crying, then you have likely gone through something that has been difficult, perhaps ushering chaos and confusion into your world. You do not know why God has brought you here. Tears come from the circumstances and events we have lived through: abuse, the loss of a loved one, sudden calamities, betrayal, and feelings that God has let you down.

It is possible that you cry because your future does not look hopeful. You think your job is going to be terminated; you have no hope for your marriage and you despair so badly that you do not even want to wake up and face the day.

You say, "I have prayed. I have asked God for help. But the help doesn't come, so what do I do?"

You go and live, crying the whole time if you have to! Do not quit doing what you know you have to do. George MacDonald said, "Bethink thee of something that thou oughtest to do, and go to do it, if it be but the sweeping of a room, or the preparing of a meal, or a visit to a friend. Heed not thy feelings: Do thy work."

There is a Bible to be read today,

>By God I am going to read it.

There is a God who "is" and I will seek Him,

>Though He seems to be so far away.

There is a God who will not forsake me,

>And I will trust Him.

Preach to yourself and say,

>"I don't know how…

I don't know when ...

    I just know this; I will not die in this low place.

I will reach my high places.

    My feet will be like the deer and I will stand on the summit,

    And God will have His glory.

I am not going to stop here.

    I refuse to stay here in this painful place."

SOWING MEANS YOU HAVE ALREADY WON

    Sowing in tears means you are not enslaved by your past or paralyzed by fear of your future. By sowing you are saying that, "I'm not bound." By sowing you are saying that you are free from the fatalism that says change is impossible. By sowing you are declaring that your destiny will not be determined by your past.

    In tears Jesus sowed in Gethsemane and look at His harvest! Have a determined faith that says, "I am not going to stop because it is hard. I am not giving up because I feel betrayed.

    There is a prayer meeting to go to – I will sow my seeds there!

    There is a life to be lived – I will sow my seeds and live!

The past has been hard ...

    The future may look bleak ...

    But God is in control!"

This I know by the Word of God,

Even Now ...

The greater the suffering the greater the comfort.

God assures me,

The greater the night the greater the light.

Paul confirmed,

The greater the weakness the greater the power.

The saints through history all proved,

The greater the loneliness the greater the presence of God.

GET UP!

TIME IS WASTING ...

HOW LONG WILL YOU PUT IT OFF?

Time slips away and can not be retrieved. The misuse of time is the greatest crime! Soon those who have been sowing in tears will burst into the forefront.

Look ahead! Quit looking back. Lesser vessels would not have survived your testimony. God knows what is about to spring forth. Just imagine what good things are coming! Your heart should be thumping. You are about to step into the harvest of your life.

Do not ever wish for somebody else's life or that you lived at another time. You were created for this moment! This moment was created for you!

Authors note: the context of this chapter is based on the assumption that there is proper sowing. According to Galatians 6, one can sow to the Spirit and reap life, but another can sow to the flesh and reap corruption.

Chapter 6

EVEN NOW ... WHEN I HAVE LOST ALL HOPE

Make Me Thy Fuel

From prayer that asks that I may be
Sheltered from winds that beat on Thee,
From fearing when I should aspire,
From faltering when I should climb higher,
From silken self, O Captain, free
They soldier who would follow Thee.

From subtle love of softening things,
From easy choices, weakenings,
Not thus are spirits fortified,
Not this way went the Crucified,
From all that dims Thy Calvary,
O Lamb of God, deliver me.

Give me the love that leads the way,
The faith that nothing can dismay,
The hope no disappointments tire,
The passion that will burn like fire,
Let me not sink to be a clod:
Make me Thy fuel, Flame of God.

— Amy Carmichael

Accepting the will of God

To accept the will of God never leads to the miserable feeling that it is useless to strive any more. God does not ask for the dull, weak, sleepy acquiescence of indolence. He asks for something vivid and strong. He asks us to co-operate with Him, actively willing what He wills, our only aim His glory. To accept in this sense is to come with all the desire of the mind unto the place which the Lord shall choose, and to minister in the name of the Lord our God there – not otherwhere. Where the things of God are concerned, acceptance always means the happy choice of mind and heart of that which He appoints, because (for the present) it is His good and acceptable and perfect will.

— Amy Carmichael

What a strange title. How can there be an "Even Now" to hold onto when you have lost all hope? If all hope is gone, then it is ludicrous to tell you to hang in there. You have no hope; how can you look forward to anything? So what is my point? Am I toying with your feelings or being sarcastic with your faith? Absolutely not!

All my life I have heard people say, "I have no hope." I have even said, innumerable times, "All my hope is gone." "So what is the point," you ask? Well, I am glad you asked that! The point is this. There are times in our lives when our hearts can no longer hope. We have no solution ... no way out. We are doomed! It is then that God comes to us and gives us what we do not have! The God of hope comes and gives us the gift of hope!

Mary and Martha were out of solutions; they did not even have a suggestion to give Jesus. It was then that the God of hope came and gave them what they no longer had – Hope!

Even though we have lost hope, God has not. That is the point of this book. With us things are usually hopeless, but with God there is always hope!

We run out of answers; God never does!

We are powerless; God is Almighty.

I want you to know, even when you have lost all hope, that the God of hope can still do something, even though you cannot!

WHAT KIND OF HOPE DOES GOD GIVE

And how do we know He is the God of hope? We know because He is the joyful God. Where there is hope there is joy! When hope is gone there can only be despair. But when there is hope then there must be joy, and God not only has joy and hope; He is joy and hope – He is the fountain by which both spring forth!

"Hope" to the Christian is "certainty." Devotion to Christ produces a religious experience that gives certainty to hope. Hope does not arise from the individual's desires or wishes but from God, who is Himself the believer's hope: "My hope is in You" (Ps 39:7). In Romans 8:24-25 and Hebrews 11:1,7, we see that genuine hope is not wishful thinking but a firm assurance about things that are unseen and still in the future.

Hope distinguishes the Christian from the unbeliever because the unbeliever has no hope. Indeed, a Christian is one in whom hope resides because God resides in him. Christian hope comes from God: His calling, His grace, His presence, His Word, and His gospel.

WHAT DOES THIS HOPE LOOK LIKE

So what does it mean that He is the God of hope? Just ask the woman caught in adultery. Surely her hopes vanished as the men dragged her from the bed of sin. She saw them picking up the stones, tools of her execution. "This is it. I am about to die – I have no appeal," she must have thought. Hope did not come from within her, it came to her. Jesus silenced her accusers. Though she could have been legally executed, Jesus forgave her – she was forgiven and free to go! That is hope!

Throughout history God has brought hope to men ... all men: both sinful men and righteous men. His hope is very real and satisfying. He satisfied the woman at the well from her thirst. For all who are reading this, consider how the God of hope has broken in upon our lives lifting us and delivering us from despair:

Even Now ...

He has healed our broken hearts.

He has delivered us from bondage.

He has healed us.

He has bound up our broken hearts.

He has brought us peace.

He has answered when we cried.

He has rescued us when we were in trouble.

He has changed our mourning into dancing.

He has given us joy and praise for the spirit of heaviness.

What kind of God is He, and what kind of people are we if He can only sustain us on the mountain tops? If we are only happy when the world is happy, if we only rejoice when the world rejoices, then what kind of believer are we? Because the Lord is our God, we should rejoice in good times or bad. We should demonstrate the greatest when things are the bleakest.

As Christians we remain in a world where there is:

Pain

Heartache

Sickness

Sorrow

Hardship

Even death

This is where our mettle is tested and where our faith is proven. We will not find hope in this world because this world is sentenced and cursed. We must look for hope that is out of this world, a heavenly hope!

LET GOD COME TO YOU WITH HOPE

An "Even Now" situation is not limited to the passing of a loved one or a feeling of abandonment by God. An "Even Now" moment is any tragedy or circumstance that makes you feel hopeless. Those times when your dreams become nightmares and visions have slipped away. It is so important that you are able to say in the midst of any situation, "Even Now, I still believe you God – Even Now!"

I have served as pastor for over two decades; no one has ever told me, "The really deep lessons of my life have come through times of ease and comfort." Instead, those who display spiritual maturity have confessed, "My progress and maturity in Christ have come through suffering." Personally I can testify that God has taught me the most while He allowed me to be tested. I have learned Jesus in suffering and trial, and I can sincerely thank God for the faith and intimacy He has given me in Jesus Christ!

Paul declared that he learned to rejoice in weakness, knowing that in his weakness God's power rested upon him. Imagine a man saying that he is strongest when he is the weakest. We have to let God teach us that lesson. God wants His power to be our reality, and we must learn to submit to God as He brings us to those points of weakness.

What we mistakenly do is question the means by which God demonstrates His power through our life, and that is our problem.

To make us strong, God will allow us to become weak.

To make us rich, He will make us poor.

This method makes no sense to us, but God's ways are not our ways. For example, because Jesus loved Lazarus, He remained where He was for days and allowed Lazarus to suffer in pain and agony, eventually dying. Jesus did that because He loved him! And as we are seeing, it is in these confusing circumstances that God will show His power and glory.

God's desire for Lazarus and his family was not suffering. God wanted to reveal His power and glory to this family; therefore, this was the way it had to be. Because we know the outcome (Lazarus was raised from the dead) we can rejoice in God. But when you, as Martha, still have to face your "sealed tombs" and wonder what God is doing; then the situation is most distressing and hopeless.

GOD IS BRINGING HIS LIFE OUT OF US

Paul said to the believers in Corinth that God is handing us over to death that the life of Jesus in us, would be manifest (2 Cor. 4:10)! The means by which the indwelling life of Jesus is to be powerfully demonstrated through us is by God's handing us over to death. And what seems more hopeless than death? But to us, this just does not seem right and so we resist the working of God. However, this is the way of the cross ... the way of life ... the way of God. It is through what appears to be defeat that God brings victory – this is the way God chooses. He makes the weak strong. So if you will not let Him make you weak, then He will not make you strong! His power is perfected in weakness!

God's power is perfected in those who have no confidence in themselves. God not only allows but can also engineer the circumstances of our life to press us into low places that seem hopeless. In these low places you must be able to trust God and say, "Even Now ...I have hope in You!"

THE TESTIMONY OF HISTORY

John Bunyan was in the Bedford jail. He could have been released if he had agreed not to preach. He struggled. He had a wife and four children that depended on him. What was he to do? Could he trust God and suffer the agony of imprisonment? Surely he could. He did. But it was not easy. His daughter Mary was blind. She was ten when he was put in jail in 1660. The burden his wife would have to bear and the absence of comfort he so longed to give to Mary was the most grueling test of all:

> The parting with my wife and poor children hath often been to me in this place as the pulling of the Flesh from my bones ... not only because I am somewhat too fond of these great Mercies, but also because I ... often brought to my mind the many hardships, miseries and wants that my poor Family was like to meet with should I be taken from them, especially my poor blind child, who lay nearer my heart than all I had besides; Oh the thoughts of the hardship I thought my Blind one might go under, would break my heart to pieces (Grace Abounding to the Chief of Sinners [Hertfordshire: Evangelical Press, 1978],123).

But broken Bunyan saw treasures he would probably not have seen had he not chosen that road with Christ.

> I never had in all my life so great an inlet into the Word of God as now [in prison]. The Scriptures that I saw nothing in before are made in this place to shine upon me. Jesus Christ also was never more real and apparent than now. Here I have seen him and felt him indeed ... I have seen [such things] here that I am persuaded I shall never in this world be able to express ... Being very tender of me, [God] hath not suffered me to be molested, but would with one scripture and another strengthen me against all; insomuch that I have often said, were it lawful I could pray for greater trouble for the greater comfort's sake (Grace Abounding, 123).

In the 1700's he served as the missionary to the American Indians of New York, Pennsylvania, and New Jersey. His was a short and afflicted life: His father died when he was nine, his mother when he was fourteen. And David Brainerd's life was cut short at the age of twenty nine, due to tuberculosis. The whole of his missionary life he coughed up blood with painful spasms – God did not heal him. He suffered relentless attacks of depression. He recorded in his diary,

> Tuesday, May 6, 1746. enjoyed some spirit and courage in my work: was in a good measure free from melancholy: Blessed be God for freedom from this death" (Jonathan Edwards, The Life of David Brainerd, The Works of Jonathan Edwards, Vol 7, Norman Pettit, ed. [New Haven: Yale University Press, 1985], 390).

David was expelled from Yale a year before graduation for saying that one of his tutors had no more grace than a chair; he was never allowed to get his degree. He never married and felt keenly the loneliness of the wilderness. Again he writes,

> "Wednesday, May 18, 1743. I have no fellow Christian to whom I might unbosom myself and lay open my spiritual sorrows and with whom I might take sweet counsel in conversation about heavenly things and join in social prayer" (207).
> "Tuesday, May 8, 1744. My heart sometimes was ready to sink with the thought of my work, and going alone in the wilderness. I knew not where" (248).
> "Most of my diet consists of boiled corn, hasty pudding, etc. I lodge on a bundle of straw, and my labor is extremely difficult: I have little appearance of success to comfort me ... I have taken many considerable journeys ... and yet God has never suffered one of my bones to be broken ... though I have often been exposed to cold and hunger in the wilderness ... have frequently been lost in the woods ... Blessed be God that has preserved me" (484).
> "When I really enjoy God, I feel my desires of him the more insatiable and my thirstings after holiness the more unquenchable ... Oh, for holiness! Oh, for more of God in my soul! Oh, this pleasing pain! It makes my soul press after God ... Oh, that I might not loiter on my heavenly journey!" (186).

God took this pain-wracked, moody, lonely, compulsive, struggling young lover of God and used him to lead several hundred Indians to eternal glory, to spark the founding of Princeton and to inflame two hundred years of missionaries with his radically dedicated four-year missionary life. Rising above his hardships, serving the "Even Now" God, he became a missionary and changed the face of history. William Carey had Brainerd's Life with him in India, Henry Martyn in Persia, Robert M'Cheyne in Scotland, David Livingstone in Africa, and Jim Elliot in Ecuador.

The testimonies abound from Christian history of those who refused to allow low times to rob them of their hope in God. In the most severe trials, believers learned to rely upon the "Even Now" God, and they saw His glory. By their own admission they began to magnify God in the midst of the pain. They learned to thank God for the pain. This is hard for most people to understand, but they thanked God for the suffering, the prisons.

In the 1600's the Episcopalians gained power over the Scottish Church. Samuel Rutherford, the Scottish minister, unable to conform to the Episcopalian ways, was imprisoned in Aberdeen. It is marvelous, the things he wrote of Christ from that prison. He wrote 220 letters which were radiant with the glory and all-sufficiency of Christ.

As they were bringing him to prison, he considered it an honor to suffer for Christ calling his cell the palace of a king, "I go to my King's palace at Aberdeen; tongue, pen, and wit cannot express my joy." There in prison he made a great discovery about the source of his joyful hope. He expressed it in these stunning words:

> If God had told me some time ago that He was about to make me as happy as I could be in this world, and then had told me that He should begin by crippling me in all my limbs, and removing me for all my usual sources of enjoyment, I should have thought it a very strange mode of accomplishing His purpose. And yet, how is His wisdom manifest even in this! For if you should see a man shut up in a closed room, idolizing a set of lamps and rejoicing in their light, and you wished to make him truly happy, you would begin by

blowing out all his lamps; and then throw open the shutters to let in the light of heaven.

What a way to turn low places in our lives into places of absolute glory and victory! This is what God wants to do for everyone. If you will look away from every depressing thing that wants to haunt you and lift up your eyes to your Almighty God, then hope will come to you. If you would really believe that He has no plans for your defeat, then hopelessness will be defeated and you will begin rejoicing and thanking God like Rutherford and Bunyan. If you can believe it, God will display His power and glory for you! I don't know how He will do it; I just believe He will do it!

CHAPTER 7

EVEN NOW ... WHEN SIN HAS DESTROYED MY FUTURE

Faith must act. If you really believe then you must do what God says!
When you seek God regarding life's trials:
    Depression ...
        Loneliness ...
            Defeat ...
                Peril ... and you say to God,
"Lord ... I believe all things are possible with you,"
    Then God is going to speak to you.
        He is going to tell you what to do.
    It is one thing to say the words, "I believe..." and another thing to believe.

Many are passive by nature.
We prefer to have Jesus roll the stone away than do it ourselves;
    Choosing rather to sit and watch the events unfold.

We had much rather someone else venture out in obedience ...
    Put their faith on the line ...
        Than do it ourselves.

Maybe we do this because we are afraid of looking foolish,
    But whatever the reasons we make for a lack of action,
        All excuses can be traced to this one thing – UNBELIEF.
Regardless of what you call it,
    If it has no action it is not FAITH!

I know someone is going to read this and say, "Sure I can see how God could help people who suffer. I can see God rescuing those in peril or showing up for those who have lost all hope, but are you going to try to tell me there is an "Even Now" for someone who has fallen in sin? How can the fallen sinner expect good from God? I mean, there are consequences, right? I do not deserve God's help; therefore, how can I expect it?"

What is more tragic than sin? Sin wrecks everything and robs us of all confidence with God. Sin incurs the wrath of God. How then can we anticipate His favor and help? Sin is deplorable; but let's face it. If God is not an "Even Now" God in regard to sin, then who in the world has any expectancy of God to deliver. Who can look forward to good? And no, I am not just talking about the "good" of going to heaven when you die. I am talking about good in this life – in spite of the crimes you have committed against a Holy God. I rejoicingly declare, in the face of sin, to all who have fallen, to all children of God who have sunk into the dregs of guilt because of personal sin and failure, "Even Now" … God is able to produce incredible things out of your life!

There is never a moment more critical than the moment of sin. If you have sinned, Satan can use it to destroy you. You face no moment more critical than now, and you must put action to your faith! You must do exactly what God has said. If you choose any course of action except the one God has given, then it will prove to be the most foolish decision, plunging you into despair and the most miserable loss of everything. By faith in the "Even Now" God, you must overcome the guilt and condemnation that sin brings. Sin attacks your heart. According to John, when our hearts condemn us we have no confidence before God. But thank God, John also says, that God is greater than our heart! We know the torment of the condemning heart. Overwhelmed with shame we try to talk with God, "Oh God please don't let anybody find out." Or we wail, "Oh God help me! Forgive me God ... the public humiliation, the loss of my testimony; the shame that I brought you ... Oh God is there hope for me anymore?"

It is not the lies that Satan brings against us that affect us the most; we know they are lies. It is the truth that Satan uses against us that floods us with guilt, depression, and shame; making us feel like giving up and thinking that we cannot go on anymore.

A PROMISING FUTURE FOR SIMON

God has spared no cost in an effort to reaffirm to all how He is the "Even Now" God, even with sin.

In one of those rare moments when Jesus was alone with His disciples, He asked them, "Who do you say that I am?"

And Simon Peter answered and said, "Thou art the Christ, the Son of the living God."

And Jesus answered and said unto him, "Blessed art thou, Simon Barjona: for flesh and blood hath not revealed *it* unto thee, but my Father which is in heaven. And I say also unto thee, That thou art Peter, and upon this rock I will build my church; and the gates of hell shall not prevail against it. And I will give unto thee the keys of the kingdom of heaven: and whatsoever thou shalt bind on earth shall be bound in heaven: and whatsoever thou shalt loose on earth shall be loosed in heaven" (Matthew 16: 16-19).

What a promising future Jesus laid out for Simon. Jesus promised him a brand new life and power. Jesus assured Simon that he will no longer be the same person. Simon was transformed in such a way that he would need to be given a new name. Simon became Peter, which means he would no longer be weak but strong; he would no longer be a fishermen, but somebody endowed with authority to effect the whole earth! Jesus gives him the authority to reach up into heaven by saying, "Whatsoever thou shalt bind on earth shall be bound in heaven: and whatsoever thou shalt loose on earth shall be loosed in heaven." This is an incredible future. But what did Simon do with these promises? He sinned! He sinned horribly, and the Bible reveals the whole sordid ordeal.

SATAN WANTS TO SIFT SIMON

Not long after these promises were made to Simon, Jesus (Luke 22) came to the moment of his crucifixion. At the table of communion Jesus turned to Simon and said, "... Simon, Simon, behold, Satan hath desired *to have* you, that he may sift *you* as wheat: But I have prayed for thee, that thy faith fail not: and when thou art converted, strengthen thy brethren." But Peter responded, "Lord, I am ready to go with thee, both into prison, and to death." Jesus then replied, "I tell thee, Peter, the cock shall not crow this day, before that thou shalt thrice deny that thou knowest me" (Luke 22:31 – 34).

You have to admit this was a very strange conversation between Jesus and the man he previously said was blessed with power to move heaven and earth. Now Jesus was telling the same man that he was going to deny him. Simon was about to face the most awful moment of his life. Satan desired to sift him as wheat.

As Satan desired Job, he now sought to attack Simon. Jesus explained to Simon that Satan requested this permission to sift and attack his faith. Imagine that!

If I were Simon I would have probably said, "What did you say Jesus? Certainly you told him no – right? Certainly you told Satan he could not even touch Simon."

And Jesus' response would be surprising, "No, actually, Simon, I told him he could. I said, 'Yes.'"

Jesus told Simon that he would be Peter. Jesus prophesied that because He knew how to transform Simon into Peter. Jesus knows what it takes to make every one of us into the person He wants us to be. Now please understand, Jesus did not need Simon to sin in order to make him Peter. Jesus was simply able to work "all things together" for good in regard to Simon because he loved Jesus. Simon had to come to his end if Peter was to come forth. So Jesus allowed him to be sifted. You see, Simon sat at the table and told Jesus that He was wrong. Simon actually told Jesus, "You are wrong about me. I would never deny you. That is not the kind of man that I am." Because Simon would not listen to Jesus and humble himself, then Jesus allowed Simon to walk into Satan's sifting. However, Jesus would never give up on Simon but committed him to prayer. God is so awesome that He could use the sin of man and the schemes of the devil as a process to fulfill His wonderful promises!

SIMON IS TOO WEAK TO PRAY

According to Mark (Mark 14), Jesus and Simon left the upper room retreating to the place of prayer. This would be the last stop that Jesus would make with His disciples before He was betrayed into the hands of evil men, falsely accused, illegally tried, and then crucified.

Earlier Peter said he was ready to go with Jesus to death. As with Simon, it is so typical for us to boast of extreme commitment when we do not have to display it, "I will die for you!" The real test of our loyalty is living for Jesus when we can. It is so easy to say we will die for Him, but can we pray with Him for one hour? If Simon could not pray with Jesus, how could he die with Jesus?

Again Simon does not hear the Lord. Jesus, stained with blood from the great agony of the night, woke Peter and told him, "Watch and pray lest you enter into temptation." But Peter went back to sleep. Jesus returned and again found Simon sleeping. He woke him and warned Simon of the coming danger. This occurred three times until Jesus said, "Take your rest. It is enough. The hour has come and the Son of Man is betrayed into the hands of sinners."

SIMON DENIES JESUS

Luke takes us before the religious leaders where Jesus is falsely accused of crimes. Trailing behind in the shadows of the night Simon followed watching the unfolding events concerning Jesus. The blood in Simon's veins must have felt like ice as he watched the horrid abuse and ridicule meted out on the Savior he so adored.

Even Now ...

Simon's world was collapsing. Confusion had caused all reason to vacate his thinking. The prince of darkness, seething into position, was crouched to attack. Simon was going down.

> And when they had kindled a fire in the midst of the hall, and were set down together, Peter sat down among them. But a certain maid beheld him as he sat by the fire, and earnestly looked upon him, and said, This man was also with him. And he denied him, saying, Woman, I know him not. And after a little while another saw him, and said, Thou art also of them. And Peter said, Man, I am not. And about the space of one hour after another confidently affirmed, saying, Of a truth this fellow also was with him: for he is a Galilean. And Peter said, Man, I know not what thou sayest. And immediately, while he yet spake, the cock crew. And the Lord turned, and looked upon Peter. And Peter remembered the word of the Lord, how he had said unto him, Before the cock crow, thou shalt deny me thrice. And Peter went out, and wept bitterly (Luke 22:55 – 62).

Luke said Simon "wept bitterly". These words are not found anywhere else in the New Testament. No one in the New Testament weeps like Peter does this night. Luke discloses that Peter violently wailed because of his sin. He was affected to his core by what he had done to Jesus. He had butchered his testimony. He had denied and abandoned the one he believed was the Son of God. Simon was violently out of control; a destroyed human, drowning in agony. Satan was grinding him out, sifting him to nothing. It was not Simon's first denial that caused him to remember what Jesus said. It was not Simon's second denial that caused him to remember what Jesus said.

It was Simon's third denial, when the rooster crowed, that caused him to remember Jesus' prophecy. It was in that exact moment, as the rooster crowed, that Jesus turned and looked at Peter.

THE SAVIOR WHO CAN DEFEAT SIN

Now dear sinner, please consider Jesus in this moment. The sinless Son of God is here to redeem us from sin. Slandered by false accusers, whipped, mocked, spat on, dragged through the night from one court to the next, Jesus is tired. He prayed the whole night with such intensity that His sweat became blood. Jesus is exhausted. The gravity of this moment is pre-eminent. Of all the days He ever lived, of all the trials He ever faced, of all of the causes He ever fulfilled, of all the prophecies that had been accomplished – this day of crucifixion was the most severe and critical of all days. On this day of crucifixion He would bear the sins of the world. He would lay His life down for the whole world. He would bring redemption. This day His heel would be bruised, but He would crush the enemy's head. This day it would be finished. He would die. He would be crucified. He would die for the sins of the world. He came for this moment.

Imagine all of that upon Jesus' mind, and before Him is the illegal court ... the false accusers. Jesus heard the accusations being hurled against him, but notice what was on Jesus' mind! He stood in the Roman court, faced his accusers, and when the rooster crowed, Jesus turned to look at Simon. Simon, the sinner, was on His mind! That is amazing love to me. The thing on His heart and mind in this most crucial day was the sifted disciple. When Jesus heard the rooster he turned and looked upon Peter. Peter looked upon Jesus.

I can only imagine what was going on in the mind of Peter as Jesus stared at him. We know that Peter was devastated for he went out and wept bitterly. Perhaps Peter realized, "I'm not the man I thought I was. I thought I was loyal, but I am not loyal. I thought I was courageous, but I am not courageous. I thought I could die with him; but I cannot even admit that I know Him, much less die for him. I am not faithful. I am not true. I am not devoted. I am not the man I thought I was." Violently shaken up, Peter disappears into the night.

Certainly Jesus was thinking something as He looked at Peter. Jesus' gaze said something to Peter. I believe this is what Jesus wanted to tell Peter in that moment, "Peter you are shocked. This morning you discovered things about yourself. Now you realize that you're not a good man. Painfully you have come to see that you are not loyal, courageous, faithful, or holy. You are not the man you thought you were. You are not the man you want to be. However, the good news is that you are the man I thought you were. You are surprised, but I'm not. You are shocked, but I'm not. Your behavior has destroyed all of your confidence in yourself, but your behavior has not destroyed one ounce of my confidence to transform you into Peter!"

WE MUST COME TO THE END OF OURSELVES

The hardest thing we have to realize is that we are not the people we think we are. We fight because we want to salvage something about our life. We work to find something good in us and then spend all our energy trying to protect it, so we can show God that there is something good about us. And as with Peter, Jesus has to allow us to be sifted that we may realize there is nothing good in us. So much of our misery comes from trying to preserve something we consider good about ourselves. Oh the freedom to let it go!

The "Even Now" God will allow you to fail where you think you never will so that you can finally become what God wants to make you. As long as you demand that you are something other than God says you are, then God will never make you the person He wants you to be. If you demand, "I will never deny you. If all forsake you, I will go with you to death." Then God has to bring you to the end of that self-confidence.

What is so wonderful about this story is that it reveals the extent to which Jesus knows us inside and out. He knows us completely. He knows we really are not what we think we are. He knows everything we have done. He knows everything we are doing. He knows everything we will do. Knowing all about us He still picked up our lives and chose us to be His. He picked up our broken, marred, sinful lives and said I can make you into something beautiful. He told Simon that He could make him Peter. Jesus also promises to give you a new name.

Just as Jesus assured Simon Peter, He assures you, "I can! I can do it! I can redeem your life. I can conform you to my image - I can

Even Now ...

do it! I have counted the cost. I know what it's going to take to build you. I know the enemy, his strength and power; but I possess all power. Sin and Satan cannot beat Me. I can do it! I am the King, I have made the decision. I am the builder; I have taken on the project. You are my project. You will never fall so far that My grace cannot reach you."

He perfects us. He completes us. He is the God of hope!

SIMON HAS BECOME PETER

John finishes the story of the sifted disciple and the "Even Now" Savior (John 21). Knowing the difficulty Peter is in, Jesus told the women at the tomb to go tell the disciples and Peter to meet Him in Galilee (Mark 16). Jesus suddenly appeared to the disciples in a locked room. Peter was there, but he was quiet and somewhat distant. Days, perhaps weeks later, Simon Peter told the disciples that he was going back to fishing. He did not say he was taking a couple of days off. He was leaving and going back to the boats. He was going back to what he was before he started walking with Jesus. Like many believers who have fallen in sin, he could only conclude that it was over. What could he possibly do for Jesus? He had publicly denied the Lord, forsaken him, and brought Him shame; so he was going back to fishing. James and John went with him. They caught nothing throughout the night. When the morning was come, Jesus stood on the shore. Realizing who it was, John told Peter that it was Jesus on the shore.

Peter could not compose himself anymore. This guilt was killing him and he knew that he had to get back to Jesus. Casting himself into the sea, Peter swam to Jesus.

Jesus said, "Simon son of Jonas lovest thou me more than these?" In other words, "Do you love me more than this fishing business? Do you love me more than this life that I brought you out of three years ago? Do you love me more than this?"

And Peter said, "Yes, Lord, you know that I like you!"

Jesus said to him the second time, "Simon, *son* of Jonas, lovest thou me?"

And Peter said again, "Yes, Lord; You know that I like You."

Once again Jesus asks Peter, "Simon, *son* of Jonas, do you just like me?"

Now Peter was grieved because Jesus said to him the third time, "Do you like me?" And he said unto him, "Lord, thou knowest all things; thou knowest that I love thee."

Jesus saith unto him, "Feed my sheep."

Peter said, "Lord you know all things. You know that I love you."

Oh how wonderful! You see a new man here. This is no longer Simon but Peter. Peter is saying, "I am not the same man anymore. I am not pretending anymore. I am not playing anymore. That man is dead. He died the night I went out and wept bitterly. I sinned against you and have disgraced you bringing shame upon you. I want to tell you that I love you just like I wanted to tell you that I would die for you, but I have learned. So, Jesus, you know. Lord, thou knowest all things!"

DON'T LET SIN DETERMINE YOUR FUTURE, LET JESUS

I do want to help those who are distraught because of sin. Do you fear that you have ruined your future, maybe wondering, "Will I ever be free? Have I ruined my future? Is God finished with me? I just don't feel like I could ever serve the Lord again?" Just as with Peter, "Even Now," if you love Jesus then follow Jesus! Jesus says to all of us, "You let me determine your future, not you ... not your sin ... not your guilt; let Me determine your future! You just love Me; that is all you can do!

When Jesus said, "Simon you are Peter," then it was done. Jesus was going to see to it that it was done. He will complete what He started in you; He will perfect you. That tells me that I must refuse to get bogged down wherever I am because wherever I am is not the last place that I'll be. God who delivered Simon and made him Peter will deliver me and make me what He has spoken over my life. He promised me a new name; He will do it!

Look at Peter, again! What do you see now? You see that Jesus did it! He transformed Simon into Peter. See him filled with the Holy Ghost, a leader within the church, an author of epistles, the lover of God who was so transformed by the blood of Jesus that he was never more the coward, proving it by giving his life on a cross. Though Simon's sifting was horrible, in the end he was a joyful blessed man in Jesus Christ, carrying the authority Jesus promised. Simon's prophetic future became a reality, Simon bar Jonah became Peter. It was fulfilled, not by any effort on Simon's part, but by the sovereign work of Jesus Christ!

Can God do anything with your life? Absolutely! Dare you sit there with sin and attempt to determine your destiny! Do not sit there listening to Satan and your feelings that it is all over for you. In Christ there is redemption. In Christ there is power. In Christ there is freedom. Let Jesus raise you up. Let Jesus deliver you. Listen to the words of the "Even Now" God as He says,

> Who forgiveth all thine iniquities; who healeth all thy diseases; Who redeemeth thy life from destruction; who crowneth thee with lovingkindness and tender mercies; For as the heaven is high above the earth, so great is his mercy toward them that fear him. As far as the east is from the west, so far hath he removed our transgressions from us. Like as a father pitieth his children, so the LORD pitieth them that fear him. For he knoweth our frame; he remembereth that we are dust (Ps 103:3-4, 11-14).
>
> This I recall to my mind, therefore have I hope. It is of the LORD'S mercies that we are not consumed, because his compassions fail not. They are new every morning: great is thy faithfulness. The LORD is my portion, saith my soul; therefore will I hope in him. The LORD is good unto them that wait for him, to the soul that seeketh him. It is good that a man should both hope and quietly wait for the salvation of the LORD (Lam 3:21-26).

Chapter 8

EVEN NOW ... WHEN LIVING SEEMS IMPOSSIBLE

Lazarus is sick. The one man who could have made a difference did not, and Martha wants to know why.

Maybe you do, too. Maybe you've done what Martha did. Someone you love ventures near the edge of life, and you turn to Jesus for help. You, like Martha, turn to the only one who can pull a person from the ledge of death. You ask Jesus to give a hand.

Martha must have thought, "Surely he will come. Didn't he aid the paralytic? Didn't he help the leper? Didn't he give sight to the blind? And they hardly knew Jesus. Lazarus is his friend. We're like family. Doesn't Jesus come for the weekend? Doesn't he eat at our table? When he hears that Lazarus is sick, he'll be here in a heartbeat."

But he did not come. Lazarus got worse. She watched out the window. Jesus did not show. Her brother drifted in and out of consciousness. "He'll be here soon, Lazarus," she promised. "Hang on." But the knock at the door never came. Jesus never appeared. Not to help. Not to heal. Not to bury. And now, four days later, he finally shows up. The funeral is over. The body is buried, and the grave is sealed. And Martha is hurt.

Her words have been echoed in a thousand cemeteries. "If you had been here, my brother would not have died." If you were doing your part, God, my husband would have survived. If you'd done what was right, Lord, my baby would have lived. If only you'd have heard my prayer, God, my arms wouldn't be empty.

The grave unearths our view of God. Why is it that we interpret the presence of death as the absence of God? Why do we think that if the body is not healed then God is not near? Is healing the only way God demonstrates His presence?

Jesus could not bear to sit and watch the bereaved be fooled. Please understand, he didn't raise the dead for the sake of the dead. He raised the dead for the sake of the living.

"Lazarus, come out!" ...

Martha was silent as Jesus commanded. The mourners were quiet.

Even Now ...

No one stirred as Jesus stood face to face with the rock-hewn tomb
    And demanded that it release his friend.
— Max Lucado.

Martha said to Jesus, "But I know, that even now, whatsoever thou shalt ask of God, God will give it thee" (John 11:22).

As important as Martha's words were to Jesus, equally important would be the decision to obey the Lord's instruction. He told her to remove the stone! It is one thing to say that God can do anything He wants. But when God speaks to you and gives you direction, then you have to obey; you have to roll your stones away! You have to stand on the edge of mystery, with all faith in God, and believe God will do what He promised! You have to roll your stones away. There has to be an act of faith that really shows you believe God is an "Even Now" God. If you deem life impossible to live, then you have to obey God for a miracle. What other alternative do you have? Life can become unbearable, but that is everybody's story! However, the pages of history are filled with countless numbers of people who went before God and found the reason to live.

For a moment I want us to consider the absolute honesty and sincerity of the psalmist in Psalm 73. "Truly God is good to Israel, even to such as are of a clean heart." Now that's the truth. The Psalmist is about to pour out a prayer of lamentation, and due to his confusion he is very careful not to accuse God of evil. He lets us know that his feet almost slipped because he envied the prosperity of the wicked! He is trying to serve God yet he is acquainted with problems. He doesn't know why these difficulties are happening; but before he spills his emotions all over the place he begins his song with a fact, "God is good …"

In his confusion and pain, heartache and struggle, dealing with things he cannot decipher, he wants to be very careful to not impugn the character of God. So he states the one certainty he has, "Truly God is good to Israel ..." That is the truth; "... even to such as are of a clean heart." But he is wrestling with apparent injustices on God's part and confesses, "But as for me, my feet were almost gone; my steps had well nigh slipped. For I was envious at the foolish, when I saw the prosperity of the wicked. For there are no bands in their death: but their strength is firm. They are not in trouble as other men; neither are they plagued like other men."

Those other men are the righteous! When you came to Jesus did life become more difficult? Instead of things being easier, did they become complicated? Have you been acquainted with heartache, confusion, adversity, attacks, persecutions, and trials? In our pain, we forget that all people suffer. It just looks like the wicked don't suffer. It just looked like life was easier before you knew Jesus. You know that's not the truth. The truth is God is good to those that fear him and have a clean heart. But this is what it looks like; it looks like the foolish get away with everything!

I love the honesty and power of the Psalmist's prayer. He tells God, "My feet almost slipped! I almost lost it! Tempted with envy for the prosperity of the wicked, I questioned if life with God was worth the trials. I thought many times, 'What's the use? What's the point?' After all I am doing for God; I'm serving God, I'm trying to live for God, and yet there are battles. I was envious at the foolish, when I saw the prosperity of the wicked. There are no bands in their death: but their strength is firm. They are not in trouble as other men; neither are they plagued like other men. Therefore pride compasseth them about as a chain; violence covereth them as a garment."

The foolish are violent, arrogant, and proud. "Their eyes stand out with fatness: they have more than heart could wish. They are corrupt, and speak wickedly concerning oppression: they speak loftily. They set their mouth against the heavens, and their tongue walketh through the earth." They take God's name in vain. The wicked behave as though they were God; they answer to no one. "Therefore his people return hither: and waters of a full cup are wrung out to them. And they say, "How doeth God know? And is there knowledge in the Most High? Behold, these are ungodly, who prosper in the world; they increase in riches" (Psalms 73:11-12). Well, why not? It's their world! The world blesses them to keep them in deception and bondage.

The Psalmist, with his feet almost slipped, says, "Verily I have cleansed my heart in vain, and washed my hands in innocency." Have you ever felt that way? You've been here, you have struggled with this. You know ... quietly ... privately before God, when no one was around, no one looking, no one listening ... your heart cried, "Is it really worth it? Is this Christianity really worth it? Is Jesus Christ really worth it?" The Psalmist too, asks if all is in vain. He cries out, "For all the day long I have been plagued, and chastened every morning. If I say, I will speak thus; behold, I should offend against the generation of thy children."

You too may wonder, "Have I cleaned my heart in vain? Why do the wicked prosper? If I ask Christians, what will they think about me? I will offend them; they'll call me a heathen and a reprobate, and scorn me; I will upset the people of God." But these are real struggles and I thank God that the Psalmist didn't give up on finding an answer! Though he could not turn to the people of God, he could turn to God!

The Psalmist continues, "When I thought to know this, it was too painful for me; until I went into the sanctuary of God; then understood I their end. Surely Thou didst set them in slippery places: thou castedst them down into destruction. How are they brought into desolation, as in a moment! They are utterly consumed with terrors."

In a moment their world falls apart. Everything about the wicked is an appearance, but the appearance is false! They try to convince themselves that they have it all together. But in a moment God can take all of that away! They will be stricken with terror, stricken with fears, and their end – destruction! I understood when I sat before God! God showed me! God answered the questions of my heart!

I want you to know it is not vain to trust in the Lord! We must know this when our world is filled with confusion and we are gripped with fear. When our feet are slipping and our behavior is damaging the lives of those around us, God can be trusted!

Have you ever taken a course of action that hurt other people? Many have committed sins, private sins, of which they are greatly ashamed. Many have been crushed beneath the realization of how awful they are as sinners. But what happens when personal sin affects others? Surely life must be impossible to live now! Can God help these people?

Many people have acted foolishly because of fear or sin of some kind. What life seems more impossible than the life that has injured others? Surely all have been plagued thinking, "It's over for me. I have sinned and hurt so many. My selfish behavior has brought danger into so many other lives. The best thing I could do is just give up my life; I am tired of hurting people and God. I'm tired of it. How long do people have to suffer because of me?" I want you to know that He is an "Even Now" God!

SIN IS NOT TRIVIAL

I would never want to treat sin as something trivial, suggesting that because He's an "Even Now" God, He will forgive us and everything will be fine. There are consequences to sin. Sin can bring great devastation upon us and others. David took a course of action, out of fear, that caused the death of the priesthood. Because of David dozens of people died: women, children, and even animals.

Sin has consequence. Don't ever treat disobedience lightly thinking, "I could just ask God to forgive me and everything will be fine." God will forgive; let's settle that. He will forgive, deliver, and cleanse us from sin and not remember our iniquities again. But when we choose to sin, we can set in motion a set of dangerous consequences.

DAVID ACTED IN FEAR

When David fled for his life from King Saul he took refuge with the priest in Nob. The priest discerned something queer with the situation. He is uncomfortable with David's presence. Perceiving the apprehension of the priest, David quickly informs him that he is on an urgent assignment for the King. His errand must be kept secret. David had fled King Saul with such haste that he hadn't time to prepare victuals or a sword.

David lied to the Priest! Surely David had no intention of getting anyone in trouble, but he lied so as not to raise suspicion. People are out to kill him, and he does not know who is a friend or an enemy. So, David manufactures the story. Now a servant of Saul is in the Temple. This man Doeg observed the meeting of David and the Priest and was also aware that the Priest had given David the sword of Goliath. David then quickly arose and fled that day for fear of Saul and took refuge with the king of Gath. Now these Philistines were leery of David's presence saying, "... *Is* not this David the king of the land? Did they not sing one to another of him in dances, saying, Saul hath slain his thousands, and David his ten thousands?" (1 Samuel 21:11)

Now David is really afraid. His feet are slipping! So David, out of fear, takes drastic action, "And he changed his behavior before them, and feigned himself mad in their hands, and scrabbled on the doors of the gate, and let his spittle fall down upon his beard. Then said Achish unto his servants, Lo, ye see the man is mad: wherefore then have ye brought him to me? Have I need of mad men, that ye have brought this fellow to play the mad man in my presence? shall this fellow come into my house? David therefore departed thence, and escaped to the cave Adullam: and when his brethren and all his father's house heard it, they went down thither to him" (1 Samuel 21:13 – 22:1).

David's theatrics saved his life. But fear is leading him, endangering all of those he comes into contact with. To keep his feet from slipping, God sends him some company. David is in a sad state; and God sends him four hundred men who are depressed, discontent, distressed, and in debt. David becomes their captain. It must have looked like a sorry bunch of soldiers at the time. It is funny how God gets us on the right track. David took advantage of the situation, became their captain, and transformed their lives. Because he gave them a reason to live, they would gladly give their life for David. This band of men became some of the most feared soldiers in all of history. They were David's mighty men!

A TOWN IS BUTCHERED BECAUSE OF DAVID

In the meantime, Doeg reported to Saul that the priest had assisted David. Enraged, Saul demands the death of everyone who wears a priest's clothes: Eighty-five priests were killed that day along with the town's men, women, children, and infants. Even the cattle, donkeys, and sheep were slaughtered.

When a young man from the city tells David of the destruction and death David says, "I am responsible for the death of your father's whole family. I knew Doeg would tell Saul of my meeting with the priest." David could have sunk into depression. He could have given up and said, "What is the use? Look at the devastation I have caused! Look how many people I have hurt! How can God be with me?" But instead, David determined to put his future into God's hands. He was tired of acting in fear and running from his problems. It was time to face up to everything and trust God to give the life He promised.

CAN A MAN SUCH AS DAVID WRITE A SONG TO GOD

It was in this moment that David wrote Psalm 56:

But when I am afraid, I will put my confidence in you. Yes, I will trust the promises of God. And since I am trusting him, what can mere man do to me? ... The very day I call for help, the tide of battle turns. My enemies flee! This one thing I know: God is for me! I am trusting God-oh, praise his promises! I am not afraid of anything mere man can do to me! Yes, praise his promises. I will surely do what I have promised, Lord, and thank you for your help. For you have saved me from death and my feet from slipping, so that I can walk before the Lord in the land of the living. TLB

What a wonderful Psalm. We love it. We love all of the Psalms. We find such consolation in every verse. We long to be the man David was, a man who could write such inspiring anthems to God. Now hold on; we *are* like David! We put the heroes of the Bible on pedestals imagining they were so much different than we are. But wait a minute, this David we so admire, this king of Israel, the giant slayer, the man who caused mass hysteria throughout all of the Philistines, is in a king's court pretending to be mad! His saliva and spit run down his face; he claws at the gates of the city because he is afraid! And yet this man writes a song like this, "What can mere mortals do to me?" Well, obviously he thought mere mortals could do a lot to him that day. Yet David says, "When I am afraid I will put my trust in you ... This I know, God is on my side ... what can mere mortals do to me? For you have rescued me from death; you have kept my feet from slipping ..."

It is hard to believe that the same David that had acted like a madman and fled from the king of Gath could be the David that later wrote that song. You see, when David was salivating all over himself and clawing at that gate, something inside of David was saying, "This is not me! This is not who I am. This is not what I will be." With such shame, David went before God saying, "I will not fear what mortal man can do to me! I will never be afraid like that again. God is for me. The promises of God are mine and I will not succumb to this defeat." So God sends 400 depressed men to David! Why? Because David is not depressed anymore!

Thousands of religious people would have surrounded David saying, "You are nothing but a backslider. I have heard talk like that all my life, David. You caused the death of God's priest! Your behavior has brought harm and jeopardy to people all over." But David knew that the man who clawed on a gate in Gath would never be seen again. Surely he thought, "That is not who I am."

Can a man write a song like Psalm 56 after doing something so dreadful? No, a man can't do that, but the Holy Ghost can. David tells us, "God delivers me from myself, delivers me from fear, delivers me from my sin. God kept my feet from slipping!" Before David ever had one mighty man on his side, he was transformed from a man of fear to a man of courage and fearlessness because of the promises of God! That was enough for David.

WHAT GATE ARE YOU CLAWING ON

So you are not the "always on top Christian." You find yourself struggling. You think you're unique; no one has to face the things you have faced. You sin. You are a failure. You are disgusted with yourself. You are like David clawing away at your own particular gate in your own particular prison, amidst your own particular fears. But something inside you is shouting, "This is not who I am; this is not who I will be." But can you rise up as David and say, "Even Now, God, after this fear and failure that has destroyed so many, You can do something with me." Then do it! Take all the depressed and discontented people around you and make warriors for God.

Consider the struggles of Jeremiah. It is hard to imagine the way Jeremiah speaks to God. Jeremiah thought his life was too impossible to live anymore.

> Woe is me, my mother, that thou hast borne me a man of strife and a man of contention to the whole earth! ... every one of them doth curse me ... I sat not in the assembly of the mockers, nor rejoiced; I sat alone because of thy hand: for thou hast filled me with indignation. Why is my pain perpetual, and my wound incurable, which refuseth to be healed? wilt thou be altogether unto me as a liar, and as waters that fail? ... Heal me, O LORD, and I shall be healed; save me, and I shall be saved: for thou art my praise. Behold, they say unto me, Where is the word of the LORD? let it come now. As for me, I have not hastened from being a pastor to follow thee: neither have I desired the woeful day; thou knowest: that which came out of my lips was right before thee. Be not a terror unto me: thou art my hope in the day of evil. Let them be confounded that persecute me, but let not me be confounded: let them be dismayed, but let not me be dismayed: bring upon them the day of evil, and destroy them with double destruction ...O LORD, thou hast deceived me, and I was deceived: thou art stronger than I, and hast prevailed: I am in derision daily, every one mocketh me. For since I spake, I cried out, I cried violence and spoil; because

the word of the LORD was made a reproach unto me, and a derision, daily. Then I said, I will not make mention of him, nor speak any more in his name. But his word was in mine heart as a burning fire shut up in my bones, and I was weary with forbearing, and I could not stay (Jeremiah 15:10, 17, 18; 17:14 – 18; 20:7 – 9).

Is Jeremiah through? Is the great prophet giving up? He wanted to, but God kept his feet from slipping! The living God, who lives within, stirs Jeremiah. And so He does with us; we want to quit but we can't. When we wonder if it's worth it, something within shouts, "Yes it is worth everything!"

WHY DOES GOD EXPOSE THEIR WEAKNESSES TO US

God lets us look at these men and women who have failed and fallen in sin, and we ask, "God how could they do such things?" Are we not glad that God did not put our sins in the Bible for everyone to read! It's not God's desire that we simply see their sin, but that we see His grace and power to recover fallen lives! God is not showing the sins of David in order that He might vindicate His justice. The story's objective is not to show sinners and their sin, but to demonstrate how God's mercy, grace, and power can redeem weak men and women who have fallen and fill them with His Spirit and make them Saints, great and victorious! Every one of these men will shout around the throne of God that all of the glory is to God for what He's done! He took me. He forgave me. He healed me. He delivered me. God has done all of this!

God is not exposing their lives so we can sit back and point fingers at them. God is showing that they are just like us! Every one of us would do the same thing. We are all sinners; but through David, God is able to show what He can do with every heart that turns to Him.

God took David, the murdering adulterer, and restored his life; making him great. God said to David's son Solomon, "I want you to be like your father David. He was a man after my own heart!" What

Even Now ...

an amazing confession from God about a man who was at one time a wretched sinner!

God was able to redeem Moses. Moses, a murderer himself, was used by God to give the most civil and spiritual laws of government to Israel, laws upon which other nations have built their societies.

God was able to use Abraham; he committed adultery with Sara's maid.

God was able to use Rahab; she had been a prostitute but became the great-grandmother of King David!

These are imperfect people, stained with gross sin. Paul, who considered himself to be the greatest of all sinners, never ceased to glorify the God who so completely gave him a new life.

Maybe things in your life have fallen apart. Like the Psalmist, your feet have almost slipped. But that is the testimony of us all. Every one has fought these battles and many, like David, have come to the side of victory. The truth of God has lifted us up and brought us forth.

But sadly, some people have not yet overcome. They are still scratching at the gates of their enemies, living in fear and hurting the people around them. Many sit in our churches discouraged, feet almost slipping, wondering, "Is it worth it?" Your feet are slipping. You are in such a difficult place right now. Perhaps your body is racked with pain. You might be fighting some sickness and confusion in your life. Your marriage may be falling apart ... all your friends have forsaken you and God seems so distant. And this great God wants to speak to you and let you know that every one of his children has been right where you are, and He can bring you out. Don't quit. Don't give up. "Your feet have not slipped because I didn't let them. Your faith did not fail because I didn't let it fail. I am the God who keeps you in my power!" So what do you do when everything is gone, when your life has been hit so hard that your world has been shaken? What makes you keep going when you want to quit? You trust in the Lord! You cannot sit here and live in fear the rest of your life, not when God is calling you to come with him.

When I was 13 years old, I went through a time of great affliction. I was in a horrible state of mind and spirit: very angry, bitter, and violent because I was here in this place; my feet were slipping.

The question of my heart was, "Is it worth following God? I want to know: Is this real?"

One night God stopped me and spoke to me saying, "I will let you walk away if that is your desire, but only on this condition: You tell me I am not worth it. You tell me you don't want me anymore."

Without hesitation I told God that I could not. And God set me free because I do believe him, and I do believe He's worth it, and I do love Him and He is worthy – He is worthy of me, the failure. He is worthy of David the failure. He is worthy of Abraham the failure, Sarah the failure, Hannah the failure, Mary the failure, Peter the failure, Timothy the failure, and you ... He is worthy of you.

Chapter 9

EVEN NOW ... WHEN I WANT TO QUIT!

Twice in my life I have heard Christians claim, in all seriousness, that God had forsaken them. This is impossibility. Does Christ live in us? He does. The living Christ dwells in the heart of every true believer – He in them and they in Him. There are no words which adequately describe the intimacy of this relationship. Jesus, in his last recorded prayer for those whom the Father had given Him, asked "that they may be one, as we are one, I in them and thou in me ... that the love thou hadst for me may be in them, and I may be in them" (Jn 17:23,26 NEB).

Jesus Christ, in the extremity of his agony on the cross, asked why God had forsaken Him. In becoming sin for us He experienced a terrible alienation from his Father, a sense of total dereliction. God did not and could not forsake the Son who was one with Him. He cannot and will not forsake us who are not only his sons and daughters, but also the dwelling-places of his only begotten Son. "I will never, never, never, never, never (the Greek has five negatives) leave you or forsake you," is his promise.

At times we may be overcome with a feeling of helpless forsakenness. This is surely not from the loving Father, but from the father of lies. The best way to answer that "father" is the way Jesus answered when tempted by Satan: "It is written." Take God's own promise with its five negatives and hold on.

— Elisabeth Elliot, *A Lamp For My Feet*, pp. 96-97.

There are countless promises given to us by the Lord for times when things are hard. There is one in the Old Testament, which was given first to Moses, then to Joshua: "I will never leave you or forsake you" (Deuteronomy 31:6; Joshua 1:5).

Lest we should fear that it was spoken only or specially to Joshua, the writer of a New Testament book quotes it just as if it were spoken to him and to all of us who read his book: "'I will never leave you or forsake you.' So we may say with confidence, 'The Lord is my helper'" (Psalm 118: 6-7).

Even Now ...

I like that part, "with confidence," don't you?

We are not meant to shake with fear when faced with temptations. We may look up to Him who conquered the powers of evil when He "reigned from the Tree" (Psalm 96:10, Jerome).

Those powers can never say that He did not conquer them, for He both exposed them and made a show of conquering them openly.

Therefore, we follow in procession behind a triumphant Christ! And if all our reliance is placed upon Him, we need never be defeated in spirit. Today, from hour to hour, He can and will lead us on to triumph – if we look to Him.

And if some duty or service has to be done which seems quite impossible, the same promise of help and triumph holds true. Over and over again I have seen the Lord do "impossible" things. I think He delights in the impossible!

And He delights to meet the faith of one who looks up to Him and says, "Lord, you know that I cannot do this – but I believe that you can!"

— Amy Carmichael, *Edges of His Ways:* pp. 147-148.

We are troubled on every side, yet not distressed; *we are* perplexed, but not in despair; Persecuted, but not forsaken; cast down, but not destroyed; Always bearing about in the body the dying of the Lord Jesus, that the life also of Jesus might be made manifest in our body. For we which live are alway delivered unto death for Jesus' sake, that the life also of Jesus might be made manifest in our mortal flesh (2 Corinthians 4:8 – 11).

Paul was suffering from great adversity in his life. He was troubled on every side. There were times in his life when he could not get away from problems; in every direction Satan was buffeting him. In spite of the mounting pressure and the growing adversity, Paul knew that he was not forsaken, destroyed, nor despairing. What a wonderful victory is in his life.

Certainly, Paul's victory stemmed from the fact that he understood what was to befall the follower of the Son of God. He knew that our path to heaven would be accompanied by suffering (Acts 14:22).

> "Take strength." These strong, simple words can be spiritual adrenaline for us when we need them. They were written by a man who knew what he was talking about, as he himself was in prison. He was writing to a young minister who was also suffering and evidently tempted by doubt, fear, even uncertainty of his call. The older man admonishes him very lovingly to take his share of suffering, take his share of hardship like a good soldier, and to take strength from the grace of God (2 Tim 2:1 NEB).
>
> Where shall I ever find the strength I need to get through this experience, this ordeal, this day, this week? The answer is take it! Take it from the grace which is ours already, in Christ Jesus.
>
> "Here it is,' He is saying, 'Will you have some?"
> "Yes, thank You, Lord. I'll take it."
>
> — Elisabeth Elliot, *A Lamp for My Feet*, p 46.

Paul was confident that everything that Satan could devise against him, instead of destroying him, would only manifest the life of God in him! In this Paul greatly rejoiced. You see, the means by which God's invested life, which is placed inside of believers, is going to be expressed is through adversity.

GOD KNOWS THE CONFLICT WILL TAKE ITS TOLL ON BELIEVERS

Now this is not always easy. Though we can rejoice in the outcome, the battle can be rather difficult. Paul did say that he was persecuted, cast down, troubled, and perplexed. Knowing the toll that this conflict can bring to the believer, Hebrews gives us great instruction,

> For consider him that endured such contradiction of sinners against himself, lest ye be wearied and faint in your minds (Hebrews 12:3).

Have you experienced the onslaught of the enemy to such a degree that you were about to faint in your mind? Though you may be ashamed to admit it, were there times when you were tempted to give up?

Many believers are beating themselves up over the disappointing ways they have handled their trials. If you are one of those believers, perhaps you cannot believe you were so immature. You cannot believe that you were actually tempted to faint and give up. But the fact is, you did go through! You did not faint! Maybe you did not show great faith. Perhaps you still feel ashamed. I have news for you; it is only by a miracle of God that any of us make it through!

> Now unto him that is able to keep you from falling, and to present *you* faultless before the presence of his glory with exceeding joy, To the only wise God our Saviour, *be* glory and majesty, dominion and power, both now and for ever. Amen *(Jude 1: 24-25)*.

YOU DO NOT HAVE TO GIVE UP

You have had trials. You have had difficulties. You might have felt like giving up because it seemed more than you could bear, but the fact is you didn't give up. You beat Satan! Do not let him beat you now. And if you are discovering that you are not some great saint like the heroes of the Bible, well, join the club! As a matter of fact, those heroes in the Bible, they are in the club too. Nobody is great – only God!

The fact that you're reading this is proof that you have not been overcome. Maybe you feel as though you are overcome. Maybe you're tempted to give up but the fact is you haven't.

> Cast not away therefore your confidence, which hath great recompense of reward ... But we are not of them who draw back unto perdition; but of them that believe to the saving of the soul (Hebrews 10:35 – 39).

Paul is not speaking to unbelievers in this passage for they have no confidence to throw away and no ability to draw back. Paul is encouraging believers to keep the faith, not to give up.

Are you in a difficult place right now? Do you find yourself wanting to give up? Perhaps you wonder, "Is it worth going on? Should I continue? I feel like giving up." Satan wants you to think that nobody has ever had to face what you are enduring. Yet every follower of Jesus has had to go through these adversities and trials, much like yours. We all have to come to a place in life where we have to answer the questions; "Why I'm following Jesus? Is He worth it? Why do I have to go through these things?" But you also come to the place where you know Jesus is altogether lovely, the most precious one in your life.

I would have thrown the church away ... religion away ... theology away - but I cannot throw Jesus away. He is the reason I go on.

Even Now ...

Elisabeth Elliot said,

When we begin to imagine that our own problems are so deep, so insoluble, or so unusual that no one really understands us, we delude ourselves. It is one of the many delusions of pride, for Scripture tells us not only that our High Priest, Christ, has been tempted in every way as we are, but that no temptation has ever come our way that is not common to man. There are no more new temptations than there are new sins. Our story, whatever it is, is an old one, and He who has walked the human road has entered fully into our experiences of sorrow and pain and has overcome them. He has comforted others in our situation, gone with them into the same furnaces and lions' dens, has brought them out without smell of fire or mark of tooth.

It is a bad thing to take refuge in difficulties, thus excusing ourselves from responsibility to others because we think our situation is unique. If we are willing to receive help, our Helper is standing by – sometimes in the form of another human being sent by Him qualified by Him to help us. It may be a case of our not receiving help because we were too proud to receive the kind God sent. Sometimes we really prefer to wallow.

"Ours is not a high priest unable to sympathize with our weaknesses, but one who, because of his likeness to us, has been tested every way, only without sin. Let us therefore boldly approach the throne of our gracious God, where we may receive mercy and in his grace find timely help" (Heb 4:15, 16 NEB).

At this moment you could be in the biggest fight of your life. So I beseech you, "Even Now," do not throw away your confidence. Don't be a person who draws back. Refuse to give up.

God knows we are tempted to faint. He knows there are moments when we would want to throw in the towel. He would never have told us in His Word not to faint if it were not possible! But He also said that we can know we are not of those who turn back! That is great news. I never have to live fearing, "Will I ever face something one day that makes me give up on Jesus?" I have confidence in my Lord and I will never throw it away!

Refuse to be the kind of person who gives up. You may think about giving up. You may think that you cannot go on anymore. But refuse to quit!

GOD PRESERVES HIS PEOPLE

While I was ministering in Poland, a remarkable testimony was given about a small village of believers who were caught in the cross hairs of conflict between Germany and Russia, during WWII.

In the early 1900s the Holy Ghost was poured out on a tiny community. God greatly blessed the people. During WWII, the Germans were entrenched in the mountains and the Russians were also situated in the mountains, but they were positioned opposite the Germans. This put the village of believer's right in the middle of where the battle should be fought. The people were arrested with fear. To fall into the hands of either the Germans or the Russians would be disastrous. Even if they survived the battle they would never survive the pillaging and rape that would follow. So they prayed. Thousands of believers prayed for God to preserve and protect them from destruction.

Suddenly the theater was changed. Instead of the Russians coming from the mountains, they disappeared. A week later the Russians reappeared in the mountains by the Germans. The battle was fought there and the village escaped the conflict.

Once again this same village faced peril of another sort. Still during WWII, the people were forced to work in the German factories. On a particular day, British planes dropped fliers warning the people that the factory would be bombed on a certain day. They were warned not to show up for work lest they suffer from the attack on the Germans. Unfortunately, the Germans were aware of the warning and demanded the people to work the factories that day threatening a much more cruel death if they did not show up.

A prophet in the village received a word from the Lord. He instructed the people to go to the factories and work; God was going to supernaturally protect them all.

Even Now ...

On the day of the bombing, the British actually bombed another factory. The factory where all the believers were was unharmed. Actually, the Germans had moved their soldiers and weapons from the factory that was supposed to have been bombed to another factory, and that was the exact factory that ended up being bombed!

After the war, a Russian officer came to the village to have his watch repaired. In a conversation with the watch maker, he mentioned that he had led a troop in battle there during the war. The craftsman said that he remembered the battle well.

He went on to ask the Russian officer, "We suspected that you would fight the Germans in our valley, but instead you fought them in the mountains. Why?"

To which the Russian officer replied, "I reported to my superiors that I could not fight the Germans in the valley. The night before I would lead our troops into battle a very terrifying man approached me from the valley. He informed me that there were many more like him in the valley and if we lead our troops into the valley for battle we would all be destroyed. My superiors were enraged that I would not move the troops into formation and fight, so a high ranking official took my post. The night before he was to lead the men into battle the same man came from the village and confronted my superior. My commander was given the same warning and decided to move our troop around the valley and fight the Germans in the mountains!"

My commander asked the man, "Why are you protecting the valley?"

The terrifying man responded, "The inhabitants of this village are the children of the living God. I am here to preserve them, and you will not harm them."

God is able to preserve His people. How many times do we find ourselves in adverse situations wanting to faint and give up, to throw our confidence away?

Remember Mary and Martha? Their brother Lazarus is dead. If there was ever a time to give up and quit hoping in God, this was it! Jesus didn't come and heal Lazarus. How can they have confidence in Jesus? But they did.

I pray this word from John Wesley helps you to hold fast your confidence.

Even Now ...

It is far easier to conceive than to express the unspeakable violence with which Satan urges temptation on those who are hungering and thirsting after righteousness. They see in a strong, clear light, on one hand, the desperate wickedness of their own hearts. On the other hand is the unspotted holiness to which they are called in Christ Jesus.

Many times, there is no spirit left in them. They see the depth of their total corruption and alienation from God and the height of the glory of the Holy One, and are ready to give up both faith and hope. They are nearly ready to cast away that very confidence whereby they "can do all things with Christ strengthening" them. Yet through this alone will they receive the promise.

When this assault comes, hold fast, "I know that my Redeemer lives and shall stand at the latter day upon the earth." And "I now have redemption in His blood, even the forgiveness of sins."

Thus, being filled with all peace and joy in believing, press on in the peace and joy of faith to the renewal of your whole soul in the image of the One who created you. Meanwhile, cry continually to God that you will see the prize of your high calling, not as Satan represents it but in its native beauty. Not as something that must be or you will go to hell, but as what may be to lead you to heaven.

CHAPTER 10

EVEN NOW WHEN ... I NEED A BREAKTHROUGH

Wars, earthquakes, famines, violence, drugs, child abuse, humanism, the occult, New Age ...

When world events and ideologies like these seem ominous and unsettling to us or when personal sorrows or tragedies confront us, where can we go but to the Lord? How comforting it is to know that we can always flee to Him and rest securely on our "Solid Rock." During the fearful days at the height of World War II, when the stress and strain of daily living seemed almost overwhelming, the comforting hymn "In Times Like These" was written.

The Scriptures warn that world conditions will continue to get worse as we approach the end of this age and the return of Christ. In addition, we must prepare ourselves for the difficult times that come to everyone as life progresses. We can only remain firm when we know with conviction that our God is in control and that all things are working out for our ultimate good. In the meantime, we simply grip the "Solid Rock"!

> **In times like these you need a Savior;**
>   **In times like these you need an anchor;**
> **Be very sure, be very sure your anchor holds**
>   **And grips the Solid Rock!**
> **In times like these you need the Bible;**
>   **In times like these O be not idle;**
> **Be very sure, be very sure your anchor holds**
>   **And grips the Solid Rock!**
> **In times like these I have a Savior;**
>   **In times like these I have an anchor;**
> **I'm very sure, I'm very sure my anchor holds**
>   **And grips the Solid Rock!**
> **This Rock is Jesus, yes, He's the One;**
>   **This Rock is Jesus, the only One!**
> **Be very sure, be very sure your anchor holds**
>   **And grips the Solid Rock!**
> Kenneth W. Osbeck, *Amazing Grace*, p. 182.

Even Now ...

Difficulties are proof contexts!

Repeatedly I am asked variations of this question: Did the Lord comfort you or were you sometimes lonely or sad? It is not an either-or thing. If I had not been lonely and sad at times, how could I have needed, received, or appreciated comfort? It is the sick who need the physician, the thirsty who need water. This is why Paul not only did not deplore his weaknesses, he "glorified" in them, for they provided the very occasions for his appropriating divine help and strength.

It was in prison that Joseph knew the presence of the Lord.

It was in the lion's den that Daniel's faith was proved.

It was in the furnace that Daniel's three friends found themselves accompanied by a fourth.

We have plenty of "proof texts" — but in order to experience their truth we have to be placed in "proof contexts." The prison, the lion's den, the furnace are where we are shown the realities, incontestably and forever.

— Elisabeth Elliot, *A Lamp For My Feet*, p. 70.

When the Philistines heard that David was king they came to destroy him. Seeing the determination of the enemy, David asked the Lord for deliverance. God assured David of victory. The great success God provided was, according to the King, the result of what the Lord did by David's hand. From this battle David called Jehovah the Lord of the Breakthrough.

Just as the village in the previous chapter needed a breakthrough from God to preserve them lest they be wiped out by the Nazis and Russians, here David is in similar distress. After years of tribulation and danger, David finally ascended the throne of Israel. God honored David; this is the Lord's doing. The Philistines did not come, however, to honor David as King. They came to destroy, just like our arch enemy Satan does to us. The enemy comes to steal, kill, and destroy. He does not come to congratulate, but to prevent us from gaining the promises of God.

God has spoken things over your life. God has given His Word and spoken emphatically about you. Just as God created the prophet Jeremiah, formed and fashioned him in the womb, and foreordained Jeremiah to preach to the nations, God has divine intentions for your life.

God prophesied over Moses' life ... Joshua's life ... Paul's life, and God has spoken over your life. God knows the prophetic intentions He has spoken over your life. Sometimes God keeps them hidden until they are ready to be revealed.

God has spoken great things about you and gives you a glimpse of those blessings. The attainment of those blessings will not occur until you are prepared to handle the revelation. Once the divine intention is revealed, Satan will attempt to prevent it in whatever way he can.

God reveals the secrets about your life when you have allowed Him to prepare you. Once you are prepared by God to take the promise, no matter what the devil does to stop you or cause you to give up, you will not draw back!

For years God was preparing David to be king – by tending sheep as a teenager, or later by fighting the bear and the lion. From a position of military prominence to the humility of being hunted like an animal – through all of these circumstances God was making David a king!

For example, when faced with Goliath, David could look back on the time he fought a bear and reckon confidently on the fact that the God who gave him power over the bear would give victory over Goliath!

God was teaching and molding David. David was taught the importance of authority and submission. When Saul was resting in the cave, it appeared God had given Saul into David's hand. David's men urged him, saying this is God's provision for you to kill Saul. God has brought the enemy to your hand David ... go kill him ... he's a demon possessed man. God doesn't want Saul on the throne; He wants you. Go, this is the opportunity of God.

But David learned that there is more to being a king than having a throne. The throne does not make a king, the king makes the throne. David knew that he would have the throne when God had finished making him a king. Then the throne would be his, not by taking Saul's life, but instead by the hand of God.

Had David heeded the desires of his men then, what would he be teaching them? Would he teach them that it is legitimate to take matters into your own hands and take a man's life when you want what he has? What do I tell 400 cut-throat outlaws when they get tired of me as King? Just kill me when you get tired of me? No. I must show them the way of God. They have to learn authority and submission. David taught his men a valuable lesson that day; God, not David, removes kings! When God puts a man on a throne, then God will take him off. Man cannot undo what God has done!

When David was ready, God put him on the throne of Israel. Just when these promises of God came to pass for David ... when finally the long awaited day arrived for David to be king, here came the Philistines! And that is just the way Satan works. Just when your promises come; so does Satan!

The Philistines did not give up because David prevailed over them one time, they came back just as Satan does. Again David inquired of the Lord. This time God said not to go after them until the sound of rustling in the tops of the trees was heard.

David did as the Lord commanded and smote the host of the Philistines. The fame of David went out to all the land, and the Lord brought the fear of David on all the nations. And as He did through David, God wants to do mighty things by your hand, causing your fame to spread to all the nations that they might know that God is with you.

GOD WILL BRING THE BREAKTHROUGH

David understood that God is the God of the breakthrough. God will bring a breakthrough for your life, but you have to believe. David could have fainted when the Philistines came against him. Sure, David was tired and weary. For years he had been living on the run. Saul was seeking his life. People betrayed him. No place was safe and never was there time to rest. And now, when God fulfills His promise, a nation comes against him in war! "Oh God I quit!" David could have said. David could have fainted and given up, but think of all that would have been lost. Think of the glory that David would have never tasted. Yes, with the promise came the devil, but victory also came; and glory! With the promise comes the adversity. And with the adversity comes the breakthrough – if you do not faint!

A BREAKTHROUGH WAS NEEDED IN BABYLON

God gave a breakthrough for Shadrach, Meshach, and Abednego! No doubt those three men and Daniel had prayed often as to how they would ever convert the Babylonians to their God? The Babylonians were steeped in pagan worship. Surely they must have pondered, "How are we going to convert these pagans to the true and living God? They won't come to our Bible studies. They never attend our church services. They don't come to hear what God is saying. They don't want to listen to us. How are we going to teach them about God?" They needed a breakthrough!

The way God wants to preach through your life is fantastic! They may not come to your Bible study, Daniel. They may not come to your service, Shadrach. But they will come to watch you burn! And, Daniel, they will come to see the lions have their way with you! It is there that I will preach to them. I will be with you in the midst of their world.

What a sermon those three Hebrews preached,

> ... our God whom we serve is able to deliver us from the burning fiery furnace, and he will deliver *us* out of thine hand, O king. But if not, be it known unto thee, O king, that we will not serve thy gods, nor worship the golden image which thou hast set up (Daniel 3:17 – 18).

"We believe in God. We love God." And for God's sake that flaming furnace receives those three lovers of God. This is a scary situation. Even the guards, who threw them into the fire, were consumed by the flames. But when the Hebrews were put into the furnace and the Babylonians looked into the fire, they saw the greatest sermon ever! The king said, "Didn't we throw three into this fire? I see four and they are all free, walking around in the midst of the fire. And the fourth man looks like the son of God."

When the three Hebrews were released from the fire, the Bible says their clothes weren't burned, their hair was not singed, and they didn't even smell like smoke!

After that sermon, Babylon knew that the God of the Hebrews was the God of gods and the Lord of all lords.

IT TAKES FAITH TO ALLOW GOD TO BREAK THROUGH FOR YOU

The promises of God sometimes come in ways we would never expect. They are wrapped in packages we do not want to open. But I encourage you to open every gift given by your Heavenly Father! "Every good and perfect gift comes down from above, from the Father of Lights, in whom there is no shadow of turning and no darkness at all" (James). Open the gift. Roll that stone away. Open that grave, and God will give you a gift today. Rahab, hang the scarlet line out your window. Hide those spies, and God will give you a gift; He will deliver you from the destruction of the city. He is the God of the breakthrough!

If you are sick, God can still break through! If all your hopes appear gone, God can break through! He can break through depression. He can raise the dead. He can make cripples walk, the blind see, and the lepers clean! He is the God of all gods! The God of the breakthrough! Whatever it is, whatever peril you sit in, He is the God that is able to break through!

He didn't break through just one time for David; He is the God of the breakthrough! For David he broke Goliath. For David He broke Saul. For David He broke through the sin of adultery and murder.

God has broken through for the saints in all ages. God broke through for Moses and Israel at the Red Sea. He broke down the walls of Jericho for Joshua. He broke through death for the Shunammite woman. God broke through the sky for Elijah and rained fire down from heaven. For Elisha He broke through the host of the Assyrian army, causing them to become blind. He is the God of the breakthrough!

Jehoshaphat did not have the power to withstand a military invasion. Though his enemies were bent on his destruction, God gave Jehoshaphat a breakthrough! For Shadrach He broke through the fire. For Daniel He broke through the lions' attack. For Sampson He broke through the Philistines and the weight of Sampson's sin. For Lazarus, God broke through death and brought him from the grave. For Paul, Silas and Peter, God broke them out of prison.

There is nothing that can prevent God from working miracles in our lives. There is no time to be depressed. How can we despair if the Lord is our God? Do you wonder, "How do I go on?" As for me, I go on because He is the God of my breakthrough! I go on because I trust Him. I may feel like fainting, but I will not! I am not of those who turn back ... I will not turn back because my God is the Lord!

Will you throw your confidence away? Some days you may be full of doubt ... but believe in the Lamb of God. Refuse to throw your confidence away! He is the God of the breakthrough! He does heal! He does deliver! He does save! He does redeem! He does come and give wisdom! He will help you financially! If you are His and He is yours, He has a plan to get you through! But you may say, "It just doesn't look good." Well don't look at your circumstances; look to Jesus! That's what Hebrews says – consider Jesus! Don't look at the problem, the imprisonment, the sickness, the besetting sins you keep bringing to the altar saying, "Well God, here I am again." God says, "I am about to break through for you. You will never be bound by this again. I am the Lord God of the breakthrough. I am going to deliver you."

Personally, I'm sick of the religion that tries to improve us. I'm sick of the religion that tries to tell us how to do it. I'm the sick of the religion that tries to hype us up and make us all excited as though we can go and change the world. It is Jesus alone who can do it and I must believe that He can do it through me!

THE KEY TO THE BREAKTHROUGH

The key to the breakthrough is knowing that God will do it by your hand! It's one thing for you to sit on the mountainside and watch God. David could just sit and say, "Well God, You're the God of the breakthrough. You are all powerful. If you really want them to know that I belong to you, then I will just sit here with my army and watch You go down there and defeat the Philistines. You do it." God could do that, couldn't He? But God did not choose to do it that way. He said, "I will do it by David's hand."

So many are running from their problems, running around scared and crying, wondering why God doesn't ever do something.

Even Now ...

Why doesn't He deliver? Why doesn't He answer my prayers? God is trying to. He is trying to get you to quit running away from your problems and your enemies. He wants you to start facing your enemy with the faith that you have in God! Trust God. Believe God. Go to your adversary and tell him he's a liar in Jesus' name! Face the situation; don't run from it. Be strong. Show them who God is!

That is what David did! "God, the Philistines have come out after me. Lord, they want me dead! Do I go out after them? Will You deliver them? Will You be with me?" And the Lord assured David, "Oh, I will David. Go out there."

God will bring victory to you; just ask Him! "God, Satan has come after me with everything he's got, there is sickness in my body, confusion in my mind, and sin in my life. Failure is all over me! God, things seem hopeless in my finances and hopeless in my family. Our nation seems hopeless. God, everything is so despairing!"

So now that you have poured this complaint out to God, what do you do? Just sit in a corner and wait for the rapture? No, go out there and face that enemy in Jesus name! Be the children of the light! Don't give up. Don't despair! Through the blood of the Lamb, God will purge all your sin. By the Holy Ghost, God will deal with all defeat and weakness! So be filled with the Spirit. Rise up and receive the forgiveness of your sins. Go forth in the power of God's might and face that antagonistic world of darkness and doom with the truth you now possess!

You will see that God will do the work, but He will do it through you. So look to God. Don't despair! Don't throw your confidence away! "Even Now," when pressed in, when cast down flat on your back, when you are scared, when you are spiritually confused; rise up and say, "Even Now," you had better not rejoice over me, my enemies. For the Lord is my light, and I shall arise! This is not the end, I am a believer! There is more, there is victory, I am more than a conqueror through Jesus, I do not know how He is going to do it, I don't know how He can do it with me. I have made the biggest mess of my life, but I know this: He will and can do it! I'm looking to Jesus to do it!"

IF YOU WANT A BREAKTHROUGH, YOU CANNOT GIVE UP

I don't care how horrible it may look, you can not give up! I don't care how tired you may be, you cannot faint! You have to go on! You have to! You have to hang in there! If sin has overwhelmed you, you have to hang in there! If you don't know why God has allowed all these things to come against you, you have to continue and believe God.

Because God is a Breakthrough God, hang in there Joseph. God is preparing a famine only you can answer. Hang in there! I know it does not look good. Sure you could doubt and sink into despair thinking, "Why are all these things happening?" Why did my brothers sell me into slavery? Why did I spend these years in a dungeon in Egypt?

Joseph, I don't know how God will get you from this prison to be Prime Minister in Egypt. I just know that He will. He is the God of the breakthrough. And praise God, He did it in one night! God took Joseph from the prison to the throne in one night! God gave a dream to Pharaoh that only Joseph could interpret.

There is Aaron worshiping a golden calf. Not only does he worship it; he made it. And he said, "Israel this is your god." As a result of this blasphemous act, we would have to assume that it is over for Aaron. After all, if we were God, we would not fool with Aaron again. But hang in there Aaron, you are worshiping a golden calf tonight, but in a few days you will be in the Holy of Holies with God. That is amazing. That is an amazing God. I have to keep believing!

Hang in there Abraham, I know you are pushing 100 years old, and Sarah is too old to have a baby; but hang in there. God will breakthrough in that womb, and she will have a son. Don't give up. Don't despair! God will still fulfill what He promised! Satan will be there to stop it in every way he can. But remember; when the promise arrives, so have you!

You have become the person who can live in the promise. You have become the person who has the faith to defy every devil who would try to stop you! God never brought David to the throne until

He made him a king. And He is not going to bring the promises into your life until He makes you the person you need to be. He will not put you in the pulpit to preach until he makes you a preacher. He will not put you in a church to pastor, until he makes you a pastor. People will put you there, but God will not – not until you are ready. Let God make you. He is the God of the breakthrough!

I will tell you a great truth. If Satan could have killed you, you would have been dead long ago. You are here today because you are preserved by God who watches over your life. You are here today believing in Jesus, having hope, because the God in heaven is the God who keeps you. He is the God who preserves you – the God who forgives you.

This is the God that we worship! He broke through the Old Covenant with the New Covenant. He broke through the Dark Ages with the Reformation. He breaks through dead religion with revivals and awakenings. He'll break through the sky with the rapture of the church. He is the God of the breakthrough! It is not over for us! Satan cannot destroy nor defeat us! He would have done it if he could have, but God keeps us and God watches over us. I don't know how, I don't know from where, I don't know who God is going to use, but I know this: if God has to move heaven and earth to fulfill his word over our life, heaven and earth will be moved! If a mountain has to be cast into the sea for God to preserve our life, then that mountain will be cast into the sea! If God has promised God will fulfill! We must believe and obey. We must refuse to faint!

Charles Spurgeon said this, "If the God you depend on were stinted in might and had a limit to His strength, then I would encourage all of you to despair. Oh! But the treasury we draw from in Jesus Christ is inexhaustible! Let Jesus move heaven and earth and His strength is not diminished! Let Him fight the host of hell in a body of flesh, to the point of exhaustion and death, and as God and He will come forth with the power to split the tomb of the dead. And not only will He come forth for Himself, but He will carry the gates of hell upon His shoulders! This is the triumph of the magnificence of our God, fully able!"

God is the God of the breakthrough. If Simon is ever to be Peter, then Simon must give way. Abram must give way to Abraham.

Even Now ...

Jacob must give way to Israel. Saul must give way to Paul. If you want to see the breakthrough of God in your life, you must give way to everything you have been and everything you are at this moment. Believe God can do in you, for you, and through you everything He promised. So get ready – a breakthrough is about to come for you!

CHAPTER 11

EVEN NOW ... IN A VALLEY

If my life is to be a crucible amid burning heat, so be it,
    But do thou sit at the furnace mouth ...
To watch the ore that nothing be lost.
    If I sin
        Willfully,
            Grievously,
                Tormentedly,
In grace take away my mourning and give me music;
    Remove my sackcloth and clothe me with beauty;
Still my sighs and fill my mouth with song.
    Then give me summer weather as a Christian
                                — A Puritan prayer.

"Some of God's wisest and strongest servants
    Are blown about like the dust of the street by fierce gusts of wind;
Yea, sometimes, it takes as much as a man of faith can do to hold his own and to
    Believe he has any part or lot in kingdom of God"
                              — Charles Spurgeon

"There is no oil without squeezing the olives,
    No wine without pressing the grapes,
No fragrance without crushing the flowers,
    And no real joy without sorrow."
                              — Unknown

Peter said we "... are kept by the power of God through faith unto salvation ready to be revealed in the last time. *Wherein ye greatly rejoice*, though now for a season, if need be, ye are in heaviness through manifold temptations ..." (1 Peter 1:5-6).

There needs to be great rejoicing. But here's the thing, Peter is not promoting some hype. People who understand that God is keeping them by His great power – greatly rejoice! It is a natural response that explodes from the certainty that God is sustaining them.

Peter also says, "...though now..." and so the rejoicing is not because you're on a mountaintop. It's not because everything in life is necessarily wonderful. You might be into day three of Lazarus and the grave, it's not looking good, and Jesus still isn't there. So, when Peter says, "Wherein you greatly rejoice though now for a season ...." thank God it's only for a season, if need be. I caution you, if you're in a time or a season of heaviness through manifold temptations then make sure you need to be! Discern, "Am I going through something by the will of God, or am I going through something Satan has designed for me?" We do not always need to go through heaviness and sorrow; we need to rebuke Satan.

Sometimes trials are ordained of God, "That the trial of your faith, being much more precious than of gold that perisheth, though it be tried with fire, might be found unto praise and honour and glory at the appearing of Jesus Christ: Whom having not seen, ye love; in whom, though now ye see him not, yet believing, ye rejoice with joy unspeakable and full of glory" (1 Peter 1:7-8).

"Even Now," why is it that you don't run away? Why is it that you don't turn your back? Why didn't you throw your confidence away? Why didn't you faint and give up? Because you love Him; that's the simple fact. You can't go away from Jesus because you love Him; "Whom having not seen you believe and rejoice with joy unspeakable and full of glory." Isn't that a wonderful faith? Isn't that a wonderful religion – a religion of joy unspeakable and full of glory? Peter is writing this to people who are going through heaviness and manifold temptations. Manifold means much, heavy, weighted.

This is the backdrop against which all of the beauty of Christ shines. There is never a greater backdrop from which we can show the worth and the value of God than when rejoicing in God while facing heavy temptation.

Let me relate Peter's exhortation to a passage in 1Kings 20. Israel has vanquished the Syrians, and they are entering a time of rest. It is at this moment that the Prophet of the Lord comes to the king of Israel and says, "Go, strengthen thyself, and mark, and see what thou doest: for at the return of the year the king of Syria will come up against thee" (1 Kings 20:22).

YOU MAY BEAT SATAN ONCE BUT HE IS COMING BACK

As Israel learned with the Syrians: Though you beat them once, they will return. The enemy is relentless. For the believer there are many conflicts fought with Satan. You fight many battles, many temptations, and many afflictions; but the Bible says, according to Peter, they're for a season if need be.

Though Satan will aggressively rage against you, there will also be moments he leaves you. However long that may be, we don't know. There is a time for trials and a time for joy. There is a time for sadness and a time for rejoicing. With the battle comes the victory, and with the affliction comes the rest.

When you are in conflict, you know what you have to do – you have to fight. But what should you do in the times of rest? It is crucial that you understand this advice. Sometimes Satan gains

Even Now ...

more advantage over you when he leaves you alone than when he is fighting you! It is in the times of peace that you let your guard down and allow spiritual disciplines to relax.

Most believers admit that times of conflict and trial produce within them great prayer, desperation for God, and seeking after God. When hell has unleashed its fury you have no choice but to seek the face of God. Every distraction has to be dismissed! Nothing can interfere with your getting hold of God: you cannot afford to let your work, your hobbies, nor your entertainments interfere. However, consider how quickly you let all of those things and more interfere with your relationship with God when everything is going well. Peter said, "... if need be." Perhaps many believers are in conflict with Satan because they squandered their times of rest and peace, and they didn't need to be in this trial.

HOW SHOULD YOU SPEND YOUR REST

> "And the servants of the king of Syria said unto him, Their gods are gods of the hills; therefore they were stronger than we; but let us fight against them in the plain, and surely we shall be stronger than they" (1 Kings 20:23).

Instead of strengthening yourself in the Lord in the time of rest, you found yourself neglecting the things of God. Do you remember how you lived in the conflict? You were not only in the prayer meeting – you prayed! Every service you were there seeking God in the altar. You even spent time fasting. You aligned yourself with believers who would pray for you.

However, in the time of peace how easy it is to neglect these matters. You missed the prayer meeting. Instead of seeking God in the altar, you quickly escape from the service to beat the crowds at the restaurant; and eventually, who comes returning? Satan! He comes to hit you, to hammer you, to be your faithful adversary! And instead of being strong, you find yourself weak; and perhaps that is what Peter meant by saying that you are in great conflict if need be!

You did not need to go through the trial, but you didn't strengthen yourself. You did not pray as you should have prayed. You were not faithful to God as you should have been faithful! You were not faithful among the people of God. You were not praying in your prayer closet. You did not have your morning devotions. You let up. And as a result, the enemy has leveled a severe blow.

I have seen this happen time and again. I have seen men who were having trouble at work and feared losing their jobs become extremely active in prayer and fellowship with the church. I have seen parents whose children were being taken by strong vices turn to God with much cries and fastings. However, once the child was recovered you rarely saw them in church or the altars again. And what happens? Satan comes back and he causes the same devastation he did the first time because God's children did not fortify their strength in the time of peace. Now our hope is in God; and though we fail to prepare ourselves in the times of peace, He is still the faithful God. When we turn to the Lord and resist Satan, he'll flee from us – again.

WHY MUST WE GO TO THE VALLEY

Peter said there will be some trials we have to face! God wants to show us His Glory. Here the Syrians accused God of only being able to give Israel victory in the mountains; God took that as a threat. What did Satan say to God about Job? He only serves you because you bless him. If you did not bless Job he would curse you! So God allowed Job to be touched because God knew the man he built, and he knew that Job would praise Him whether He had blessed him or taken things from him.

There are times we are called upon by God to enter into battle because lines have been drawn in the spiritual realm, and we have very little understanding of what is taking place. There may be something Satan charged God with, and God has chosen to defeat Satan's accusations by us! So God brings us into the conflict, not for our destruction or loss but to demonstrate His Glory and power through our lives! Let's look what God's response is to the Syrians, "Because the Syrians have said, The LORD is God of the hills, but

Even Now ...

he is not God of the valleys, therefore will I deliver all this great multitude into thine hand, and ye shall know that I am the LORD" (1 Kings 20:28).

> "I will praise you, O Lord, with all my heart. Before the 'gods' I will sing your praise. ... When I called, you answered me ..." (Psalm 138:3).

Amy Carmichael, referring to this Psalm said,

From this we understand that there are activities in the unseen world which are not explained to us. Every now and then the curtain between is drawn aside for a moment, and we see. But it is soon drawn back again.

So much we do not know.

>But this we do know:
>
>>"When I call, you answer!
>>
>>You give me strength."

If that is true, what does any present trouble matter?

>How I wish to be able, in my life, to turn all
>
>>Disappointments,
>>
>>>Setbacks,
>>>
>>>>And trials of faith and patience

The way Paul used his!

What reward, what golden treasure came to our Lord because Paul endured and was victorious in his difficult circumstances.

Everything God is doing in your life is happening so that you will know He is the Lord. God will never do anything to destroy your faith. He is not doing anything to destroy your confidence in Him. He is not doing anything to destroy your trust in Him. If you're struggling with some trial, failing to grasp what God is doing with you, and you cannot understand why God would allow this to hurt so much; then I exhort you not to throw away your confidence, and you will see the glory of God. I do not know how, I do not know who He's going to use, I do not know where it is going to come from; but I do know this: in the end of this trial you will have more confidence in God than you ever had. Do not quit. Do not give up. Do not throw your faith away. Do not faint. Do not give up your confidence that you can have in the Lord.

We can clearly recognize the analogy of the Syrian's taunting as to how Satan will seek to weaken us. Satan says, "I cannot ever take on the children of God when they're on their mountaintops. When believers are in a blessed state, and everything's great. When they are so happy. When they have their health and money. Then I cannot touch them. I cannot prevail over those who have no reason not to trust You."

Then Satan says, "We have to get those believers down from their mountaintops. If I can get them in the valley, then they would be easy prey. While on the mountain God always delivers them, but they would quickly abandon God if I could bring them into a valley! God is only their God on the mountain top; He is not their God in the valley."

Oh beloved, this is where we get to prove how wrong Satan is, and what a liar he is. Satan has such audacity to insinuate that we are only faithful to God because of the blessings. As Job, we get to show Satan that the Lord is our God in the valley too!

God was determined to show the Syrians how mighty He was in the valley. So God commanded Israel to get out of the mountain and move to the valley. There God showed that He was not only God in the mountain, but He was God in the valley as well. He is God everywhere, but so many do not know that. They confess it and hope and pray that it is true, but there are so many that really don't know that. God wants to turn their confessions into realities – He is going to answer your prayer, not by keeping you on the mountain, but by bringing you into the valley and being your mighty deliverer.

However, some cannot bear the valley. It is dark ... cold ... intimidating. It is filled with shadows and noises and places for the enemy to hide. This is why some give up and turn to man! It is so easy to sit on the mountaintop with the prophet and sing and shout that our God is the God of the valley too, but how the singing and shouting ceases when God then takes us into the valley – do we say, "Amen" then? Most of the time we begin to cry, "Wait a minute God! I like it up here in the mountain! We've got fortresses up here. We know how to fight up here!"

And God assures us, "But I know how to fight down there, and I'm going to show the enemy that the strength of Israel is not Israel, nor Israel's horses and chariots, but the Living God! I am going to show that whether on the mountain or in the valley I am in your midst!"

SATAN DOESN'T THINK WE CAN TAKE MUCH

I am sure that Satan knew God could beat him anywhere. I believe that the enemy thought it really wasn't the inability of God in the valley, but perhaps it would have been the attitude of the people of God because they were in the valley, that he could win. The enemy was counting on the people to be despondent. The enemy considered that if the people of God could fall into a little hardship, go through a little bit of a rough time, then they would lose their joy and faith in God.

How easily this valley comes into our lives. Sometimes all it takes is for someone to say that they do not like you. These valleys come when someone talks about you, slanders you, gossips about you, or hurts your feelings. Suddenly you are in the valley: you are depressed. You are having a pity party and losing touch with God. It's not that God's too weak; it's just that you are too carnal. You sulk in your depression. You sulk in your despair. You wallow in self-pity rather than rising up and taking hold of God in faith.

We must know that Jesus said, "I will never leave you nor forsake you." If you are in a valley, He is with you. As David said, "… though I walk through the valley of the shadow of death, I will fear no evil: for thou art with me; thy rod and thy staff they comfort me" (Psalm 23:4). God will be as strong in the valley as He is on the mountaintops.

My faith has got to be just as real, filled with joy unspeakable and full of glory, when I'm on the mountaintop or when I'm in the valley. However, the valley allows me the greatest opportunity to show my joy and devotion to God. When I'm as happy as I could be or when I'm fighting sadness, when I'm as joyful as I can be or when I've got the feelings of depression all over me; I have got to rejoice in the God who keeps me!

That's the truth of my love. It is easier to stand among the congregation of the Lord and sing about how much I love God, but it's on Monday where my love is proven more! My love for God is better demonstrated by saying, "No!" to the pressures of this world than saying, "Amen!" to the preachers point.

Anybody can rejoice in God on the mountaintop, but sometimes we get the opportunity to rejoice in God while in the valley. I may enjoy the mountaintop better than the valley, but the power of God is the same in both. The God who keeps me on the mountain, keeps me in the valley. The God who delivers me in the mountain, delivers me in the valley. So I can say, "Even Now, You are God in the valley!"

GOD HAS BEEN IN YOUR VALLEY BEFORE

Maybe some of you are in a valley: a valley of depression, a valley of despair, a valley of hopelessness, a valley of self-pity, a valley of unbelief, a valley of doubt. God knows the valley you are in. He knows every valley: the valley of loneliness, the valley of hurt, the valley of neglect, the valley of feeling unwanted, the valley of being betrayed, the valley of being lied about. I pray you have the faith to say, "God, today, Even Now, I will not be destroyed or defeated in this valley, for You are the strength of my life." Peter

Even Now...

said you should not think it strange concerning the fiery trial which is to try you, as though some strange thing happened to you. I'm so glad the Holy Ghost told Peter to write that because many times we all thought our trials were unique; that no one could possibly understand what we were going through.

But your trial is not unique! You're not the only one that's ever been there. You are not the first one in this valley, and you will not be the last. God has brought millions through your valley. Peter is telling you that when in the valley you need to realize that you are not alone. My God is experienced in bringing His children through this valley.

Peter says they came through rejoicing! If God did that for them, surely He will do that for you.

Now I understand that when we are heading into the valley, we do not always think this way; therefore, we must preach the truth of God to ourselves!

I'm not experiencing some brand-new situation that God has never faced before. God is not in heaven sweating it out thinking, "Oh, my angels, what am I going to do? Lee's facing something that I've never even thought of, and I don't know what to do! I don't know how to get him through it!" I am confident that the Almighty God knows what to do! Glory is coming! I can rejoice!

I want a God that I can rejoice in. Hardship for soldiers is not unusual; it is common. I am a soldier of Jesus Christ. I'm not expecting some lily-white life ... some easy life with no problems, no hardships, no heartaches, and no enemy. I have been clearly warned by my God that there will be hardships and adversity. Satan will come, or the Bible is a lie! But I also have the absolute assurance I am more than a conquer. There will never be a devil that can beat me. There will never be a legion of devils who come against me and shall prevail – "Thanks be unto God who giveth me the victory through my Lord Jesus Christ..."

So whether on the mountain or in the valley, God is going to show Himself strong. I am not going to sit down and fall into despair; I'm not going to do it. I will realize manifold temptations come, but so does glory!

Everybody in the world suffers and faces difficult trials, but only the Christian can be rewarded. I take the sufferings that I have to go through with Jesus Christ as a means of great joy and rejoicing because the weight of the suffering does not compare to the weight of the crown. And so I pass through it with a great joy in God. I'm not going to suffer like the rest of the world suffers. I'm not going to mope, complain, and be depressed like the rest of the world. I'm going to count on the faithfulness of God to keep me. I'm going to count on God to bring me through this valley.

I must preach this to myself. I can't wait for you to come preach to me, to get my attitude straight and my eyes on Jesus. I preach to myself because I've seen far too many people lose their way in the valley. I've seen far too many people stop in the valley, rather than come to the end of God's glory. I refuse to stop in it. I love it when God sends people to support me, but with or without them, I do have the Holy Ghost and the Word of God that will lead me through.

TO GET OUT OF THE VALLEY - REJOICE

To get out of the valley – rejoice. Let the enemy do his worst; God will do His best! Let the enemy bring everything he's got. It doesn't compare to the vastness of God's power. The lost cannot rejoice. Their troubles are forever; mine are for a season!

I want to surround myself with the family of God. I hear people say they just had no one to talk to. The truth is they did not want anyone to talk to. There is always help in the house of God!

You do not have to be alone; you choose to be alone. In the night of Jesus' valley, when He passed through Gethsemane, He refused to be alone. Jesus brought three men with him into prayer and told them to stay awake and watch with Him. It is the encouragement of the body of Christ that brings us through more than we know.

TO GET OUT OF THE VALLEY – BE ACTIVE

To get out of the valley – be active! Be active in season and out: pray, seek God, walk after God, and be filled with the Holy Ghost whether on the mountain or in the valley.

Even Now ...

I've rarely seen a person fall away from God on the mountaintop, but I've seen many fall from God in the valley. Let me tell you something. Not everyone makes it. Everyone does not come through. This is not because God failed. Their faith did.

Be active. The valley exists for only a season of time. The valley comes and the valley goes. The end of the valley is victory; so don't stop. Keep on walking. Though there may be a thousand reasons to give up and sit down, don't! I am not going to take time out along the way. God will give me strength; He will make me continue when the young men faint. I will mount up with wings like eagles and soar through it. I'm here to fight, and I'm here to get it over with. So let's deal with it today. My valley ends today. I'm not here to stay!

As soon as you roll that stone away, your battle will be over. As soon as Martha told the men, "Remove the stone," Lazarus came out. As soon as you move your stone, as soon as you quit saying to God, "I can't do it, God. Even though I believe You can do anything, I just don't know if I can ever get over this." As soon as you trust Him your battle is won. Why live in defeat? Get active and stand on what God has promised you; obey what He told you to do. If He said to forgive, forgive. If He said to quit worrying, quit worrying. If God said not to despair because you are to look to God, then look to God! Be done with it. Roll the stone away. Get out of this valley.

CHAPTER 12

EVEN NOW ... GOD DOES LOVE ME

If when an answer I did not expect
Comes to a prayer which I believed I truly meant, I shrink back from it;
If the burden my Lord asks me to bear be not the burden of my heart's choice,
And I fret inwardly and do not welcome His will,
Then I know nothing of Calvary love.

If I wonder why something trying is allowed,
And press for prayer that it may be removed;
If I cannot be trusted with any disappointment,
And cannot go in peace under any mystery,
Then I know nothing of Calvary love.

If I refuse to allow one who is dear to me to suffer for the sake of Christ,
If I do not see such suffering as the greatest honor that can be offered to
Any follower of the Crucified,
Then I know nothing of Calvary love.
— Amy Carmichael, *If*, pages 47-49.

> Now Jesus loved Martha, and her sister, and Lazarus. When he had heard therefore that he was sick, he abode two days still in the same place where he was (**John 11: 5 – 6**).

We started in the book of John and now we return here for the conclusion of the matter. Lazarus is dead. This grieving family sent for Jesus. They knew Jesus could heal Lazarus; after all they never saw a sickness Jesus could not heal. But Jesus did not come, at least not when they wanted Him to.

Do you believe that God is good only as long as He is doing what you want him to do, or do you believe God is good even when you are faced with circumstances that throw you into confusion, and it seems to you that God is so far away?

Questions do arise in our minds causing us to wonder why God is allowing things to spin out of control. Sometimes it even gets worse! You may say it can't get any worse and somehow it does – do you believe God is good then?

There is an amazing expression found in these passages that reveals why Jesus did not come to the family when asked. Believe it or not, it was love that kept Jesus away. Is it possible in the moments of life when we question if God loves us, that all of His actions towards us are because of love? "Now Jesus loved Martha and her sister and Lazarus ..." (John 11:5).

Surely one would think that because He loved them He would immediately go to them. After all Lazarus is sick; he is suffering; he is dying; something is taking his life. It had to be painful; it had to be unpleasant. But Jesus did not go immediately to them, yet the scriptures say that He loved them. "When He had heard therefore that he was sick, He abode two days still in the same place where He was" (John 11:6). How does love do that?

Has God withheld your desires because He loves you? Do you remember a time when you needed God? Perhaps you cried to God, "Tomorrow is too late; I need You right now!" You tell yourself, "God loves me. God is here for Me." Yet, He did not come! You need Him right now. You need Him today, but He has not come; and what you were hoping and believing for turned out badly. It really did. It appears that there is failure written over everything – that's how it appears.

That is what it looked like with Lazarus. By the time Jesus got there, Lazarus had been dead for four days. So it's over! Again, what kind of love is this? What kind of faithfulness is this? What kind of God is this who loves us so much as to allow our trials to go from bad to worse? It does not make any sense, and it is not supposed to – at least not until the end!

YOU MUST ENDURE TO THE END TO SEE THE POWER OF GOD

But some people cannot go to God's end because they give up in the process. Some people never see the conclusion that God wanted to bring because somewhere in the process of confusion, pain, and the seeming apparent neglect of God, they threw away their faith. What the loving God really wanted to do was never accomplished because they gave up. Now thank God, Martha did not give up. Martha, as soon as she heard Jesus was coming, went and met him, but Mary was still in the house.

> Then said Martha unto Jesus, Lord, if thou hadst been here, my brother had not died. But I know, that even now, whatsoever thou wilt ask of God, God will give *it* thee. Jesus saith unto her, Thy brother shall rise again. Martha saith unto him, I know that he shall rise again in the resurrection at the last day (John 11:21-24).

That's what she knew. Carefully consider her words. She was hoping in a resurrection that was future, not one for that day. An expectation of a resurrection today was not in her plans. A healing was what she wanted, but instead death came. But "Even Now" she has this faith, "But I know that even now whatsoever you will ask of God He will give it to You." That has to be our confession. We have to be able to say in the dark times of our life, "Even Now, Jesus, whatever You ask Your Father, He will give You!" When life is too painful ... too hard, when you are sure that you have come to your end, you have to look past every discouragement and look up to God and say, "Even Now, God, I am trusting You! What looks too hard for me is not too hard for You. What seems impossible for me is not impossible for You."

THE LOVE OF GOD

Let me show you how much Jesus loved Lazarus, Mary, and Martha! His love is the radiance of the whole story. Just look how His love comes bursting into their worst nightmare! Because He loved them, Jesus was building their faith!

Jesus is the author and finisher of our faith. He is the builder of our faith. He wants us to trust God! The Bible says that perfect love casts out all fear. If Jesus loves us, then He has to bring us up against our greatest fear and show Himself sufficient – so we are not afraid anymore! That is what He was doing for Mary and Martha. What did Mary and Martha struggle with? Was it sickness? No, they knew Jesus could heal the sick. It was death! That was their battle. It appeared that something occurred which took away hope, and now they could only say, "If you had been here, Lazarus wouldn't have died." "But can you believe he will live?" is what Jesus asked. You have faith that I can heal but your faith struggles with death. I allowed Lazarus to die not because I do not love you but because I love you. I am going to take your faith where it has never been before. I am about to give you confidence in Me that you have never had. By the end of the day you will not only rejoice that I can heal, but you will rejoice that I can raise the dead!

Do you think this was an easy moment for the sisters? No, this was hard for Mary and Martha. Just consider how humiliated they must have felt. Do you think for a minute that it was easy for Mary and Martha to roll Lazarus' grave stone away? Come on, they are in the middle of a funeral for a brother that has been dead for four days, and the man who did not show up when they needed Him is asking them to roll the stone away! The whole town is there. Family is there.

Surely throughout Lazarus' sickness Mary and Martha were preaching, "It is going to be fine ... we sent for Jesus ... He will come. He loves us ... He will heal Lazarus!

We saw Jesus heal the lame. We watched him open the eyes of the blind. We watched him take the lepers and heal their skin; He healed their disease! This Jesus, oh he's coming!"

They have been preaching to the family and friends about Jesus for some time, telling aunts, uncles, and cousins, "You just wait; He's our friend! Just over there in the dining room He has had many meals with us. He sleeps over there in that room. We take care of Him; and He loves us. Lazarus, we've sent for him..."

No doubt the sisters looked out of the window assuring Lazarus and their family that Jesus will be here any minute. But He never came. And when He does show up, it is at the end of the funeral! Jesus wasn't even there to help them grieve their loss. But now He comes, four days too late! You can only imagine the smirks and condescension that accompanied Jesus' presence.

ARE YOU GOING TO DO WHAT GOD ASKS

So this is the Jesus that loves them. This is the Jesus that can heal the sick ... heal cripples and open the eyes of the blind. And now He wants Mary and Martha to roll the stone away!

If family and friends are what they typically are, I am sure that somebody said to Mary and Martha, "You are not going to listen to this guy are you? He has embarrassed you once, and now He wants to open the grave! Listen, if He wanted to see Lazarus, He should have come to the wake. Tell me you are not going to do what He is asking!"

You can appreciate the faith of Mary and Martha because you see this is not an easy situation. Even when you have to defy the skeptics and every natural reason, you do it because you love God. You have to have faith to move the stones in your life. If you do not want your past to determine your future, then you have to obey God. You can live there if you choose. You can say, "I just can't get past these things in my life. I can't get over it!"

But if you ever want to be free of the molestation and abuse, the anger that rages inside of you; then you have to roll stones away in your life. God can bring you past the guilt of aborting a baby; your life doesn't have to be forever marked like that.

It is easy to say that God can forgive, but will you let Him forgive you? It is easy to say that God can do anything, but will you let Him do anything for you? Today, if you will hear His voice, He will save you!

> Blessed *be* the God and Father of our Lord Jesus Christ, which according to his abundant mercy hath begotten us again unto a lively hope by the resurrection of Jesus Christ from the dead, To an inheritance incorruptible, and undefiled, and that fadeth not away, reserved in heaven for you, Who are kept by the power of God through faith unto salvation ready to be revealed in the last time. Wherein ye greatly rejoice, though now for a season, if need be, ye are in heaviness through manifold temptations ... (*1 Peter 1:3-6*).

YOUR FAITH MUST GROW IN GOD'S POWER

Because we are kept by the power of God, our faith must grow in the power of God. Our confidence in God's power cannot simply rest on the testimonies of others or the books that men have written. We want confidence in God's power to be based soundly upon what God has said in His Word. We want our lives to act upon that Word. This is faith.

For eight years I suffered from a condition called psoriatic arthritis. It is an extremely painful form of arthritis that inflames the joints. For five years I never slept more than three hours a night as the pain would attack me. I was very diligent in asking God to heal me. After all, God declares that He is the Healer. You can only imagine the struggle I had as my condition worsened and lasted from one month to a year and to multiple years with no response from God.

He was not helping me, so it seemed. I am a preacher and my faith was attacked. My boldness to declare God's power and willingness to heal was challenged. I would think, "How can I preach that God heals and here I am sick. How can I pray for the sick with faith when my own faith has not brought healing into my own body?

Oh, how tormented I was, until one day the Holy Spirit spoke to me, "Do you believe I am the Healer?"

"Yes." I responded "You are the Healer."

He asked me, "How do you know that?"

And my heart shouted with such confidence, "Because the Bible says You are! Because You told me You are!"

Oh thank God! I was free when I went back to the Bible and not to my experience. That whole day I was elated, worshipping and praising God. I preached a most powerful message declaring that God is a healer, not because my experience says He is, but because the Word says He is, and that is enough for me. If I die with my condition, then I will die confidently preaching and declaring that God is the Healer.

It was not long after that moment that I woke up one morning to discover that I had slept for twelve hours. I rolled out of the bed and realized that there was no more pain in my body! I believe I rejoiced more because of what the Bible told me than in my own healing. How precious is the Word of God.

FOR FAITH TO GROW YOU MUST ACT

Now my confidence will grow as I act upon the surety of God's Word. It is there, in obedience to God, that I will see His hand and power! That's the kind of faith I want.

In any given church there are people who are somber, sleepy, complacent, lazy, and lacking enthusiasm in their spirit. But there are others who are excited about God. They are praising God. They don't need anybody to stimulate them! They don't need music to motivate them. They are excited about God! They praise God for God! Why? Because they walk with God! They have seen the mighty hand of God during the week!

But those that live by books, letters, and testimonies of others still live in their past. It is sad that all some people can say is, "Did you hear what God did for so and so?" But how exciting it is for one to say, "Did you hear what God did for me?"

I was ministering on death row in Angola State Penitentiary in Louisiana and there I met a truly born again man who had confidence in the power of God.

He was asked, "Suppose the governor came in here and said, 'I will let you go free on one condition. You have to recant your faith in Jesus Christ.'"

He responded, "Then I would tell that governor that I will be the first one to sign up for the death house rather than deny Jesus Christ."

Now do you think that man needs music to get him to praise God? Do you think he would look like the dead in most churches today, or would he be greatly rejoicing in the Lord?

THE SHOUT OF TRIUMPH

I am trying to stir you up to live a life of miracles – a life of no impossibilities because you walk with the God who can do anything. I am telling you that nothing is too hard for God. When we roll our stones away and see the power of God, our hearts cannot wait to shout unto God with the voice of triumph on Sunday! We enter into church with shouts of praise and joy because all week long we have been exposing ourselves to the power of God!

I am excited in the Lord because He loves me, not because I have a problem-free life! God, who loves me, triumphs for me in all my despair and affliction! He always comes through. If I will just believe Him, obey Him, and roll the stones away; then I will see His glory!

For God's people to be filled with the Holy Spirit and give God that Spirit-filled worship is the greatest need of this hour! There the Holy Ghost will fill His people; God will inhabit our praise. He will dispense His blessings as He sits enthroned upon our praise! We must praise God! We must invite his presence. We must invite His presence through the gladness of our hearts and the enthusiasm of our spirits and the confidence of our faith in the power of God.

How encouraging is the word Peter gives us, "Kept by the power of God ... wherein you greatly rejoice." There needs to be great rejoicing. But here's the thing, I believe that everybody who knows they are kept by the power of God does greatly rejoice. However, people who can not rest in the power of God can not rejoice. It is very sad to see them down, feeling abandoned and dispirited.

Peter says that the great rejoicing is in the face of manifold temptation. The rejoicing is not because you're on a mountain top. It's not because everything is wonderful and great. You might be into day three of Lazarus and the grave, all hope is practically gone, and Jesus still is not here. But we rejoice in the power of God that keeps us to the salvation that is soon to be revealed!

Martha, why are you going to listen to Jesus? Are you really going to roll the stone away? Come on Martha, you gave Jesus a chance, and He failed. No one would blame you if you told Jesus no. Thank God Martha had faith – faith in Jesus, faith in His love, and faith in His ability! She did not throw her confidence away. She did not turn back. Why? Because she believed in Him; He does love us! And she saw the glory of God!

It is a wonderful faith, a wonderful religion, where the believers rejoice with joy unspeakable and full of glory! I would not waste my life on anything less. The God of the universe loves me. Shall I not rejoice? The God of the universe has promised to keep me by His great power. Shall I not rejoice exceedingly? Loved by God ... if that is true, and it is ... then there is an expected end!

All the paths of the Lord are loving and faithful – Psalm 25:10

> All the paths. ...
> ... All does not mean "all – except the paths I am walking in now,"
> or "nearly all
> —except this especially difficult and painful path."
> All must mean all.
> So, your path with its unexplained sorrow or turmoil,

Even Now ...

    And mine with its sharp flints and briers
        and both our paths,
With their unexplained perplexity, their sheer mystery —
They are His paths,
    On which He will show himself loving and faithful.
        Nothing else; nothing less.
I am resting my heart on this word.
    It bears me up on eagle's wings.
It gives courage and song and sweetness, too –
    That sweetness of spirit which is death to lose even for a half-hour.
        ... My Father, you alone ...
        You yourself ... are enough for me.
No matter what path you lead me on today,
    It is not strange and unknown to you. ...
Only let me go with your presence!
                          — Amy Carmichael

CONTACT

Pastor Lee Shipp may be reached for ministry by contacting:

First New Testament Church
3235 Aubin Lane
Baton Rouge, La. 70816
USA

(225) 293-2222

Pastor Shipp's Email address is:
Office@fntchurch.org
ctoh@fntchurch.org

Please visit us at: www.fntchurch.org

ABOUT THE AUTHOR

Pastor Lee Shipp, as the founder and senior pastor of First New Testament Church, has ministered God's Word through the power of the Holy Spirit for over twenty years. Led by a devotion to his Savior and a love for the scriptures, God has used him to teach and preach throughout the world, through conferences, camp meetings, and revivals. Pastor Shipp is also founder and President of "A Call to the Heart"; a ministry of evangelism and outreach through radio, T.V., literature, and national and international campaigns. As well, Pastor Shipp also serves on the Board of Directors for "The School of Christ International." Pastor Shipp and his family live in Baton Rouge, Louisiana where they continue to serve the Lord with their church family.

www.fntchurch.org